Subliminal P

Learn How to Influence People's Unconscious Mind to Do Anything You Want with Subliminal Persuasion and Dark NLP in Relationships, Parenting and at Work

Joe Silva

Table of Contents

Introduction

The following chapters will discuss techniques that you can use to get people to do what you want in your personal life and in your career. What's unique about the techniques we discuss here is that they are subconscious—you will be able to influence people without it ever occurring to them that you are, indeed, influencing them.

We will look at what subliminal psychology is, and we will explain how you can deploy it in a different scenario to your benefit. We will look at the specific techniques you can use when dealing with your partner or your spouse, with your children, and even with your coworkers and your boss.

For each technique that we discuss, we will give a real-world example of how it can be used, which should make it easy for you to understand and master each technique.

We will look at the concept of neuro-linguistic programming, and we will explain how it works. We will also delve into the dark side of NLP and teach you the secret techniques used to program and to control people. We will explain how you can make people more suggestible so they give you what you want.

We will look at how to psychoanalyze people. When you understand a person's psychological makeup, it becomes easier for you to figure out which influence techniques will work best with him, so we will also discuss how you can understand a person's motivations—and even how you can predict the way he or she is going to react under certain circumstances.

There are lots of books on subliminal psychology in the market right now, so thank you very much for choosing this one! Every effort was made to ensure this book was filled with useful and practical information. Please enjoy!

Chapter 1: What Is Subliminal Psychology?

When the word 'subliminal' comes up in everyday conversations, it's almost always about 'subliminal advertising' or 'subliminal messaging,' which have been the subject of much debate for a few decades now. As far back as the 1950s, there have been claims that savvy advertisers and politicians have the ability to get the masses to purchase certain products or to adopt certain political views by flashing messages on TV.

There have been hundreds of iterations of conspiracy theories about this subject since then, and even today, you can find lots of online communities and social media groups patronized by paranoid people who are afraid of being exposed to subliminal messages. Subliminal psychology works—but not in the way that most people assume. For example, the idea of "subliminal advertising" turned out to be a hoax, and there is a lot of evidence that shows that it's not really possible to coerce the masses into buying certain products or adapting certain political viewpoints just by flashing brief messages over the screen.

Even if that were the case, most Western countries have regulations that prohibit the use of underhanded methods to 'brainwash' people through mass media, so there's no need for the tinfoil hat. However, what you need to understand is that subliminal psychology can be usedand *is* being usedto influence people every day in interpersonal relationships. To understand how this works, let's look at the science behind the concept.

Subliminal messages are passed across using "subliminal stimuli." Subliminal stimuli are sensory stimuli—just like any other that you might come across daily. They can be visual or auditory stimuli, or they can be related to your sense of smell, taste, or touch. The difference between subliminal stimuli and ordinary stimuli is in how long you are exposed to the stimuli.

The term "subliminal" is used in reference to one's conscious perception. When you are exposed to subliminal stimuli, it means the duration of the exposure doesn't rise to the level of your conscious perception. In other words, you aren't exposed to the stimulus long enough for it to get to the threshold where it registers in your conscious mind. Let's take the example of a garden-variety visual stimulus to help you understand this concept.

Supposing you look at a picture of a celebrity you are familiar with—the image will be taken in through the eye and the optical nerve into the brain, and the brain will register the fact you are looking at that picture, and the person's name may even pop into your mind.

Scientists believe it takes up to 13 milliseconds for your brain to consciously perceive a visual stimulus, which means if you are exposed to that same image for less than the requisite 13 milliseconds, it might not register in your conscious mind that you have seen the image. However, subconsciously, your mind will perceive the image, and this will elicit some form of reaction, which will happen without your awareness; if it's someone you like, you'll experience a good feeling.

Subliminal messaging works, but in a very mild way; evidence shows that it stimulates mild emotional activity in the person who is exposed to the stimulus. Understanding this point is very crucial if you want to understand how to use it to your advantage in personal relationships. When people are exposed to subliminal messages, they may experience a mild and fleeting emotional reaction to the stimulus, but they won't be coerced by it. To put this into perspective, you can use subliminal stimuli to make someone have a brief warm feeling towards you, but you can't use it to make him addicted to a consumer product or to turn him into a mindless robot. So, if the subliminal message is a stimulus that's introduced to a person when she is inside a store, she might feel a strong urge to buy a particular product, but she won't be "compelled" to prefer that product forever.

So, if you study subliminal psychology, you will realize that the conspiracy theorists were somewhat right, it's just that they lacked a sense of proportionality in the way they viewed the concept. Subliminal messaging works not by influencing the masses to take certain actions or to believe certain things; it works by slightly altering people's emotions for short periods of time.

Subliminal messaging can be used in relationships, in friendships, and even in the workplace to influence the behavior of others to one's own benefit. In the real world, this concept is more often referred to as "subconscious priming." Subliminal messaging and subconscious priming refer to pretty much the same thing because they both involve influencing people using certain stimuli without their conscious knowledge. However, practitioners in the field of psychology seem to prefer using the term "subconscious priming" because "subliminal messaging" has a lot of negative connotations thanks to the controversy that has surrounded it for decades. In this book, we will use those two terms interchangeably to refer to the same thing.

The subconscious mind plays a greater role in the decisions that we make in our daily lives than we will ever realize; we decide whether to trust strangers, or whether we are attracted to certain people within seconds of meeting them without it ever registering in our conscious minds. That means understanding subliminal psychology is the best way to influence the way people perceive you because it works on an instinctual level. If you master the art of subconscious priming, then you will be able to use it to your benefit in your daily life.

In the next few chapters, we will look at how subliminal messaging can be used in different kinds of personal and professional relationships to achieve certain predictable outcomes. We will look at how things like eye contact, social touching, and several other techniques can be used as stimuli to make people perceive you a certain way, and how these stimuli can open the door and allow you to influence people in a number of ways.

Chapter 2: How to Use Subliminal Psychology in Relationships

Subliminal psychology can be a potent tool in relationships, particularly during the courting stages of the relationship. When you are in a relationship with someone, there are two ways you can benefit from a deep understanding of subliminal psychology.

First, you can be able to use subliminal messages to influence the person you are dating. Second, if you have a keen understanding subliminal messaging, you could be able to read the person to understand the kind of thoughts, emotions, and desires that they are hiding—and you can then facilitate them to open up, thus strengthening your relationship.

When we talked about subliminal messages, we pointed out that the subconscious mind has the ability to pick up on messages that the conscious mind isn't even aware of. What we failed to mention is the mechanism with which the brain picks up those subliminal messages is, for all intents and purposes, a two-way street: the subconscious brain can send out subliminal messages without the conscious brain knowing it. If you are in a relationship with someone, or if you are trying to get into one, you can benefit immensely from learning to pay attention to the subliminal messages others put out.

Cold Reading in Relationships

The subliminal messages people put out can be observed and understood using a process known as cold reading. Cold reading is a technique that has been used for millennia by psychics, clairvoyants, gypsies, conmen, magicians, and all sorts of people.

Before the general public came to understand that cold reading is something that any observant person could do, there was a widespread belief that people who could cold-read others had some sort of supernatural ability. Today, we know that cold reading isn't at all magical or supernatural. Psychics and clairvoyants are just people who have trained themselves to pick up the subliminal signals that others put out. Let's look at how you, too, can acquire this skill and use it to thrive in the world of dating and relationships.

At the beginning of the relationship, and even during the course of a considerably longer relationship, the other person will require you to be a great conversationalist, a seducer, and someone who is able to meet their emotional needs. They say the key to any good relationship is open communications, but even people who communicate openly as a matter of general principle, tend to hold back certain things; unfortunately, those are the things that really count. Your strategy should be to get as much information out of the other person through open and honest conversation, but you need to be able to supplement that information with cold reading.

When you cold-read your partner in a relationship, you won't be doing it with malicious intent. Of course, there are some "pickup artists" and manipulative people who prey on others in relationships, but that doesn't mean cold reading skills can't be used for the mutual benefit of both people in the relationship. You can use cold reading to put the other person at ease on the first date or to connect at a deeper level with your spouse or partner.

In order to cold read people in relationships, you first have to make them feel comfortable enough to express genuine emotions. When people feel uneasy, or they are afraid, it's hard to read them at a deeper level. You have to present yourself as charismatic and confident.

You have to converse with them in a way that indicates that you understand them, that you value them, and that you are willing to pay attention to them. Also, since you want them to open up, you need to express intimacy without making them uncomfortable. Of all those qualities that you have to exhibit, remember that intimacy is the most important one. In relationships, intimacy can be about sex, but it's a lot more than that. Other than sex, real intimacy requires romance and sensuality. Most importantly, intimacy requires you to express a "natural vibe" that conveys honesty. It's not something that is easily faked, so if you want to be able to cold-read your partner or someone in whom you are romantically interested, the only way to get them to lower their defenses is to present your genuine self to them.

Let's say you are out on a first date, and you are trying to cold-read your date and pick up on the subliminal signs that he/she is putting out. You will first start by building rapport between the two of you. Later in the book, when we talk about neuro-linguistic programming, we will discuss ways to build rapport by mirroring other people's body language.

You need to start with a light topic of conversation because you want to understand what the other person is like in general before you can dive deeper and uncover information that can help you win their hearts.

As you progress with the small talk, you need to pay keen attention to your date's body language. When you talk to people, and they are at ease (meaning that they are in a neutral emotional state), you will be able to tell from both their verbal language and their nonverbal signals, what things are most important to them. Our verbal and nonverbal cues vary depending on our emotional states, so you can tell how certain topics of conversation affect your date emotionally.

You might notice that when your date talks about his/her job, their manner of talking or their body language differs from their baseline or neutral emotional state (say, for example, when they are talking about the weather or the ambiance of the restaurant you are in). That slight variation in body language, together with their word choices, can tell you whether your date is passionate about their job, or whether they find their job suffocating.

When you pay your date a compliment, their reactions can offer you a lot of subconscious signals that you can use to cold-read them. You can also let your date steer the conversation however they like, and you can then collect as much information about them as possible. When you cold-read someone, you are trying to gain an understanding of who they are within, and how they are likely to react when subjected to certain emotional states. Unlike the psychics and exhibitionists, your end goal is not to put on a show for an audience. It is to learn all you can about the other person. However, to successfully cold-read your date, you will still have to use some of the tricks employed by exhibitionists.

The most important trick in cold reading is elicitation. Elicitation refers to the art of getting people to voluntarily give you private information without raising alarms in their minds. Elicitation is similar to fishing for information but in a subtle way so that the other person doesn't feel like you are prying.

Of course, when you are on a date, there are questions that the other person would naturally expect you to ask, but since you want to know more than the basics, you will have to elicit the information from them. One way to elicit information is by concealing questions as statements. When you ask a lot of questions during a date, the other person will feel like they are being put under a microscope, and that might be off-putting. If you want to cold-read your date, you don't want to disenchant them, so you have to find a way of turning those prying questions into statements.

For example, instead of asking questions like, "Where did you grow up? How many siblings did you have? What were your parents like?" You could use statements to get your date to talk about all those things. You could merely say something like, "I bet you had a happy childhood." Your date will take this as an invitation to reminisce about their childhood, and you will learn a lot without making him/her feel like they are being interrogated.

Using statements instead of questions also helps to ensure that the conversation flows smoothly. As social beings, we are wired to reciprocate both in words and actions. So, if you keep asking questions, even if your date is willing to answer those questions, he or she will try to keep those answers as brief as possible before returning the same questions to you; remember you want them to keep talking about themselves, not asking about you.

Subliminal Persuasion in Relationships

After you cold-read a person, and you have all the information you need, you can use subliminal persuasion on them. If it's someone you have just started dating, the subliminal persuasion might not have as high a success rate as you may hope because, even if you are a decent cold-reader, it's still hard to completely figure someone out after just a few interactions.

However, if it's someone you are married to, or if you have been dating for a while, you would have had plenty of time to figure them out, so you can deploy subliminal persuasion techniques in a more effective way.

To subliminally persuade someone, you need to have a way with words. It's really an art form; you have to weave your intentions into conversations in such a way that they are less likely to be detected, but at the same time, you want to make sure you increase your odds of getting a positive response when you express your intentions. For example, let's say that you are trying to get your partner or spouse to go visit your parents in the near future. Now, you know that this is a topic that they are unlikely to warm up to. So, when you exercise subliminal persuasion, you have to bring up the topic in such a way that it makes it rather difficult for them to shoot it down outright. Instead of asking your partner, "Do you want to go visit my parents?" you should ask, "When are we going to visit my parents?"

If you ask the first question, your partner has the freedom to say "No," and if he is not too fond of your folks, he is going to exercise that freedom, then he will bombard you with dozens of excuses to validate his response.

However, if you frame the question the second way, you are priming your partner to say yes. It will register in his mind that "going to see your parents" is a foregone conclusion, so he can only bargain on the questions of "when." In some cases, if your partner is a really forgetful person (maybe because he is always busy with work or he often drinks and forgets the promises he makes) he may truly believe that he already agreed to go see your folks, and he will react accordingly. Before you know it, you will be moving things around in your calendar and trying to figure out which weekend is most suitable for a trip back home.

Another subliminal persuasion technique involves the use of the power of suggestion. The power of suggestion is a real and powerful thing, and it's an effortless way to prime someone into behaving in a particular way. Someone tells you that they are ants all over the place, and you start filling itchy, as though bugs are crawling all over your body.

The fact is our perceptions are subjective, and since our brains are wired to exist in codependent communities, sometimes we can subconsciously substitute our own judgment for the judgment of other people. This is even more likely to happen when we are dealing with people we trust; our parents, siblings, relatives, friends, partners, colleagues, etc. As a child, when your mother said, "Put on a sweater, as it's cold out," you would suddenly notice how cold it was, even if you were just fine a moment ago. When you are dating someone or are married to them, you will have some good rapport between the two of you, and that puts you in a unique position to effectively influence them using the power of suggestion.

The power of suggestion can be explained using a concept called "response expectancies." This concept theorizes that the manner in which we anticipate our responses to particular situations ends up influencing the way we respond to those situations. In order to put it simply, once your brain expects something to happen, your own thoughts, behaviors, and reactions will start to contribute towards making your expectation a reality.

To use the power of suggestion, you have to make subtle propositions to the person you are dating to get them to start anticipating the outcome that you want. When you are picking up someone on a date, and you say, "I have a good feeling about tonight," their whole experience that night will be a lot better than it would have been and they may even be open to things they hadn't planned to do that night. That's because, in their subconscious minds, they have been subliminally primed to expect a great date, so, without realizing it, they work hard to make that date great.

Chapter 3: How to Use Subliminal Psychology in Parenting

No matter the age of your kids, subliminal psychology can help you be a better parent to them. From the time they are born, children are naturally conditioned to trust their parents. That's because as babies and as toddlers, they are entirely dependent on their parents for survival. However, as children begin to understand the world around them, they begin to exercise independence by using their own judgment. The older they get, the more independent they become. That is just the natural progression of things.

Before we look at the subliminal psychology techniques that you can use on your kids, we have to make it very clear; your aim should not be to control your kids. It should be to instill good values in them and to teach them to exercise their independence in a smart way. No matter how "bratty" your six-year-old is being at the moment, and no matter how rebellious your teenager has become lately, you have to understand that whatever action you take when dealing with the child, it's going to stick with him/her forever. Don't be shortsighted. Think of the long-term impact of your actions and subliminal psychology strategies; don't deploy a strategy that could potentially scar your kids for life.

That being said, children, even at a very young age, can be a handful, and you need a lot of subliminal psychology tools in your arsenal. In this chapter, let's discuss some tricks parents have used with some considerable level of success. Feel free to try some of them out with your own kids, and see how it goes. Getting children in line is no easy task, but sometimes, you can get them to change their attitudes and do whatever you want. How? With reverse psychology. Reverse psychology techniques are subliminal in the sense that when they are correctly used, they fly under the radar; it doesn't register in the mind of the child that he is being tricked.

When you are dealing with toddlers who are scared of something, you can make them less afraid by creating a fictitious solution to whatever they are afraid of. Toddlers tend to be very imaginative, but when that imagination runs amuck, it can become problematic. The kid may want to sleep in your bed every night because he is afraid of monsters. He may throw a tantrum at the doctor's office because he is scared of getting a shot. All parents have different ways of dealing with such situations, but some methods are universal; the Tooth Fairy was invented to make kids less afraid of having their teeth pulled out.

Toddlers are at an age where they are just beginning to understand the world around them, and they tend to create wild stories to explain the things that they don't yet fully understand. As a parent, you can try to plant more fun versions of fantastical stories in place of the horror stories the kids tell themselves. You can use reverse psychology to teach kids to shake it off when they get hurt in the playground. When your kid falls when running outside in the lawn, or when they accidentally get hit by a ball, don't be quick to display empathy. If you are playing with him and he falls, just carry on with the activity and disregard the fall. You will be amazed to see that the child quickly forgets the pain, and he gets back to enjoying himself. If you treat every little incident as if it were an emergency, you will condition your child to become an attention seeker.

No. We are not advising you to turn into a terrible parent who ignores the child when he is seriously injured and needs first aid or consolation. You should learn to make a quick judgment about the extent of the injury the child has incurred, and then you should proceed to ignore those harmless falls. You also need to learn to tell why your toddler is crying. When you are dealing with babies, you must attend to them every time they cry. However, with toddlers, you have to learn to tell whether they are crying to get attention, or whether they are in real pain.

As a point of caution, even if your child cries out of real pain, you should avoid using treats to console them, and instead, you should try to address the real issue. Treats can create a feedback loop in your child's brain, which can be dangerous and can lead to a lifetime of bad habits.

For instance, let's say your child gets hurt when running around the house, and he starts crying. You decide to console him by offering him a scoop of ice-cream. If you do this several times, his mind will start associating the pain with the ice-cream, so the next time he merely bumps onto a piece of furniture, he's going to scream at the top of his lungs to make sure you notice.

When your kid gets hurt after you have performed first aid and made sure that he is physically alright, let it be a lesson to him.

His brain will associate the pain with the clumsy action that he took, and he will be more careful next time. Don't interfere with that natural learning process by rewarding him with a treat.

Another way to deal with children using subliminal psychology is by giving them the illusion of choice. This may sound diabolical, but it works well, especially with younger kids (7 years or younger). If you try this trick with older kids, they will see through your game, and they may turn things around on you. Here is a simple example of how the illusion of choice works: Supposing every time you take your kid to the park, he wants to stay there longer than you can afford to let him. You have tons of things on your schedule, and you want to go back home, but he throws a tantrum, and it puts you in a difficult position.

Next time, when you want to leave the park in a few minutes, call the kid over and instead of asking him to get into the car, offer him a choice. Tell him, "you can keep playing with your friends, but we have to go soon. How much more time do you need to spend playing? Five minutes, or ten minutes?"

Now, the little guy is going to do the 'smart' thing and answer "ten minutes." You'll then say, "OK," and let the kid keep playing.

Remember, the kid can't tell time yet, so in a few minutes, you can call him over again and tell him, "Okay, I gave you all the ten minutes you needed. Now, let's go!" He will happily follow you to the car because it was his own decision.

There are very many variations of this trick that you can use in everyday situations. Just like adults, kids like to feel like they have a choice, and as long as you manage the illusion in a way that doesn't insult the child's intelligence, you could get him to do lots of things with little resistance. You can get your child to make choices that are more responsible by suggesting to them that it's the "grown-up" thing to do. Every little boy aspires to be a "big boy," and every little girl wants to be treated like a "big girl." You can tell your kid, "Big boys clean their rooms," or "Big girls spread their beds," and because they are eager to be perceived as "grownups" they'll try to show some initiative.

One parent came up with a trick to get her little kids to eat vegetables. She would prepare meals for the whole family and set everything on the table. She would serve the meals, but fail to put vegetables on the children's plates – only adults would get the vegetables. She would then make "yummy" noises when eating her veggies, and this would get the kids a bit curious. After a while, the kids wouldstart asking, "Mummy, what's that?"

"This is grown-up food," she would say, "but I suppose I could let you have just a little bit." The children would jump at the opportunity to have a taste of the 'grown-up' food.

This way, she trained her kids to enjoy vegetables. It wasn't that the kids liked the taste of the vegetables; they were just glad they were part of the "grownup club." By the time they were old enough to figure out it was just a trick, eating vegetables had become a habit that was ingrained in them.

You can also use the classic reverse psychology technique where you pose a challenge to the child so that he has to prove you wrong. The next time you want the kid to put all his toys away, don't ask him directly. If you say, "Can you please put your toys back into the chest?" you'll be met with a resounding "no." However, if you say, "I bet you can't put your toys back into the chest—no way can you do it," the kid will take it as a game, and he'll play it to win. If your child has a competitive streak, you can use it to get him to do a lot of things. You can make it a kind of sport for him, and you can even time him to make him do things faster.

Subliminal Parenting Techniques When Dealing with Older Kids

Tweens and teenagers have a better understanding of the world around them, so the little tricks we have discussed thus far won't work on them. In fact, when you are raising teenagers, you will spend much more time dealing with the subliminal machinations that they put in motion, so you need to focus on learning techniques that can help you counter those machinations. Reverse psychology can work on teenagers to some extent but remember they are not as susceptible as they may have been a few years ago. Your teenage kids are going to rebel in one way or another. That is natural; they are facing an identity crisis, and as they try to figure out who they are, they'll try different things. As a parent, you have to decide what "hill you want to die on" when you are trying to cope with your child's rebellious phase. You can give your teenagers the leeway to rebel in certain areas, so that they perceive you as reasonable, and not oppressive. That way, when you finally draw the line, they'll be more inclined to see things your way because after all, you have been fairly lenient with them. However, for this to work, you have to make sure that your kid understands that you are, in fact, making a concession. For example, if your teenager decides to dye her hair to some strange shade of green, don't panic. It's not a gateway to her joining a gang—it's an opportunity for you to negotiate new boundaries with her.

The first thing you need to do at this point is to get in her face and make a big fuss about her new hair color. She may try to tell you to "chill out" (or whatever kids say these days) but make sure that you express all the worries you can think of. Remember, whether or not you are truly worried that is beside the point; you are trying to get her to see that this is a big deal for you.

After the initial confrontation, you should wait for some time; maybe wait until later in the evening, after everyone has calmed down. You should then go to her and apologize. Say that you are sorry you overreacted and that as a parent, you just want the best for her. Tell her that deep within, you know that her choice of hair color is an expression of her individuality and you respect that. At this point, if you are a half-decent actor (or if you are expressing real emotions), your teenager will recognize the fact that you have made a concession; that you have treated her as an adult, and that despite your own fears, you have decided to trust her judgment. She will want to encourage that attitude in you because that's what teenagers really want; to be thought of as grownups who can exercise good judgment. She will be glad you have offered her something, and her brain will be primed to reciprocate. That is when you strike!

Tell her, "I'm still a little worried because I hear these horror stories about kids changing their looks, and then they end up doing drugs. Please, promise me I am right about you, that you wouldn't turn out to be one of those kids, because I can't bear the thought of something like that happening to you."

Your teenager won't think that you are asking too much of her at this point; not after that 'big' concession that you have just made. She will seek to reassure you that she won't do drugs. And, if you raised a half-decent kid, she will truly mean it. We can't promise that she won't succumb to peer pressure at some point in the future, but that promise she made to you will weigh heavily on her, and it may just be the source of the willpower she needs when temptation comes knocking.

Chapter 4: Using Subliminal Psychology to Influence People at Work

Whether you are a boss or a low-level employee, whether you work in sales, or whether you are the IT guy, there are lots of subliminal and subconscious techniques you can use to influence people at work or in business.

As we have explained, subliminal influencing involves persuading people to make specific decisions based on messages that don't register in their conscious minds. The whole concept of subliminal messaging has its origins in advertising and sales. In as much as it is applicable in romantic relationships and in parenting, it's most commonly used in business and career situations.

Because of the impersonal nature of the relationship dynamics that exists here in the workplace, employees have no qualms about manipulating their bosses into paying them more, and bosses have no qualms about manipulating their employees into becoming more productive. The social contract that governs business relationships allows for subliminal influencing—if you are not using the following techniques to your advantage, then you are at a self-imposed disadvantage.

First, let's talk about how you can get someone at work to be your friend or close acquaintance. There are always people at work who have influence, and it is advantageous for you to be close to them. It could be a colleague with whom you wish to collaborate on future projects. It could be someone within the organization, who outranks you, and you know he could help you climb up the career ladder.

Let's say that you don't know each other at a personal level; to him, you are just a person who works in the same building. Thus, how do you get him to be your close friend? Easy. Just ask him to do you a minor favor.

Walk into his office and ask him to lend you something small; maybe it's a reference book or a portable device. You could also ask to pick his brain on a matter that relates to the job. After he has done you a favor, say "thank you very much" to him in the most gracious way possible, and then leave. You have just made a friend.

From that point on, you won't just be a random face in the office; you will be someone who is of interest to him. When someone helps you with something, no matter how small it is, their brain is immediately primed to feel invested in you, and in your welfare. He may even come over to you later to see how your project is going, and if you need any further help. You can build on that, and with a little more effort, you will soon be getting what you wanted from them.

The second subliminal technique we'll discuss is one that can be used in negotiations. You may be looking to negotiate to get a higher salary, you may be quoting estimates for the funding you need for a project, or you may be selling something to a client or customer.

The trick is simple; first, ask for way more than you actually need. You can then scale back slightly as you carry on with the negotiations. This trick works because the moment you mention a high amount of money, even if it's ridiculous and unreasonable, the person with whom you are negotiating will be primed to use that number as a reference point.

This trick works for more than just number-based negotiations. It can also work for other sorts of requests. Supposing you are the boss, and you want your employees to put in a couple of hours of overtime, say on Thursday and Friday. During a staff meeting earlier in the week, you could mention that there is a lot of extra work that has to be done in the coming days, and you will require all employees to come in during the weekend.

Now, that will annoy even your most mild-mannered employees. There will be murmurs of discontentment. However, as the week progresses, you will hold a subsequent staff meeting and tell your employees you know how valuable their weekends are, and that you have assessed the workload, and you now believe that if everyone could stay a little longer on Thursday and Friday, you might be able to salvage everyone's weekend plans. Your workers will feel like that's a reasonable compromise, and they are more likely to agree to your new request.

There are many iterations of this subliminal trick, and different versions can be used to influence both individual and groups. The reason it works when it's used with colleagues with whom you are well acquainted is rather simple. If you ask someone to do you a favor and he turns you down, he will feel a stronger sense of obligation to agree to your second request (and it helps when that second request sounds like a bargain compared to the first one).

The next subliminal technique that you can use in the workplace is flattery. It is said that flattery could get you anywhere. It may seem like an obvious technique that anyone can deploy without much training, but remember that people in the workplace and in business situations tend to be sharp and vigilant, so they'll spot in genuine flattery from a mile away. Make sure the flattery comes across as honest.

People in the workplace have certain notions about themselves and their abilities. When you flatter them, you are aiming to validate those notions that they already have, and not to exaggerate because that would make them suspicious. If a colleague acts like he is the best salesman on the team, you can flatter him by 'acknowledging" it out loud.

When you flatter someone who has high self-esteem, he will like you more because he will just think you are sincere. If you flatter someone with low self-esteem, he may hold it against you because he may think you are either mocking him or you are patronizing. Make sure you understand who you are dealing with before you deploy flattery as an influencing technique.

You can use mirroring as a subliminal technique to get someone to warm up towards you before asking them to do something for you. Later in the book, when we talk about neurolinguistics programming, we will dive deeper and discuss mirroring in more detail.

However, for now, we should note that if you mirror someone's body language and verbal cues subtly during a conversation, you stand a better chance of convincing him to do you a favor. That's because mirroring helps establish a rapport between two people, and in some cases, it can make someone feel like the two of you are very close to each other; like you were kindred spirits.

You can also use fatigue to your benefit when you are trying to influence people at work or in business settings. People start making decisions early in the morning. In the course of the day, busy people can make hundreds of decisions, small and big decisions. Scientists have discovered that the more decisions people make during the day, the more their decision-making abilities are impaired. While people make well-thought-out decisions early in the morning, by late afternoon, they'll be making rash decisions without seriously weighing all the facts; this concept is called "decision fatigue."

When people get tired, it's because their energy levels are depleted. However, it's not just physical energy; it's also mental energy. When you ask people for favors when they are tired, you'll be amazed to discover they are more likely to agree to do what you want.

When you walk into a colleague's office late, close to the end of the business day, and you ask him/her to do something for you, instead of taking a moment to assess what the request is and to say "yes" or "no," he/she is more likely to tell you, "I'll look into that tomorrow." They are trying to avoid taking on anything else at that moment, but they inadvertently agree to do it at a later time. When the next day comes around, they are more like to do what you asked because they already gave their word, and most decent people are psychologically programmed to keep their promises.

When you want to ask someone for a favor at work, you can use nodding as a subliminal messaging technique to prime them to say yes. Scientists have established the fact that when the person you are conversing with nods a lot as they listen, they are more likely to agree with what you are saying.

In western societies, and in most other societies for that matter, nodding one's head (in an up and down motion) is used to indicate agreement. If you are in deep conversation with some, they are naturally inclined to mirror your body language, so if you nod a lot, they too will start nodding.

Talk to the person for a while as you nod, and when you notice that he has started copying you, you'll know it's time to slip your request into the conversation.

Even if you don't want a favor, and all you want is to convince someone to see things your way, nodding still helps. It will increase the person's level of agreeableness as it relates to you.

On a larger scale, subliminal messaging can be used to influence people in business to increase the sales of certain products, or to increase subscriptions to certain services. Stores and other businesses use music all the time to modify the shopping habits of the people who walk through their doors.

It may not seem so, but there is definitive proof that music has the ability to affect your consumption habits. Some years back, researchers in Britain sought to prove this concept. They used French songs as background music in a store for the whole day. The next day, they only played German songs. They kept alternating between French and German songs for two weeks. In the end, they analyzed the sales of French and German wine brands carried by the store.

On the days when they played French songs, French wines outsold German wines. On the days when they played German songs, German wines outsold French wines. When the customers were asked about the relationship between the music they heard and the wine they choose to buy, none of them seemed to have a clue the two were linked.

Some of the most successful supermarket chains in the world play calm, relaxing, and familiar music throughout. They program their playlists in such a way that there is no time wasted between tracks. The people who walk into the stores may be aware of the music that's playing, but they have no idea the music has the effect of making them stay longer.

Supposing you are picking the last item on your shopping list, and just as you put it into the basket, and start walking towards the cashier counter, one of your favorite classic rock songs starts playing. Studies show that in such situations, most people are more likely to walk around a bit more, enjoying the music, waiting for the track to end. As they do this, customers may find themselves tossing a few additional items into their shopping baskets – items they had no intention of buying in the first place. And what if the next song is even better than the last? Well, some customers might just decide it's a good day for a shopping spree!

Chapter 5: What Is NLP?

NLP is short for Neuro-Linguistic Programming. The concept was pioneered in the mid-1970s by a linguist and a mathematician as a way to model the communication techniques of the best communicators so that those techniques could be taught to other people.

Richard Bandler and John Grinder, the pioneers of NLP, studied three different therapists in the hope they could observe their behavior, document it, and use it to reproduce excellence in other people.

Currently, there are two major ways that psychologists, various kinds of therapists, and even amateur practitioners that look like NLP.

First, most of these people consider NLP to be a set of modeling tools which can be used to observe, to model,as well asto reproduce excellence or success in various careers fields and even in personal relationships.

The second way to look at NLP is by thinking of it as a set of processes which have been achieved over time as a result of modeling done by other practitioners.

In order to understand those two different interpretations, it is useful to think of NLP the same way you think of computer programming. When you want to get a computer to perform a particular function, you could either use a program someone else has created for that purpose, or you could write your own program to do the same thing.

In the same way, NLP practitioners can either perform their own modeling to come up with their own NLP programs or use processes other NLP experts created and standardized.

So, what is NLP good for? Well. When NLP was initially created, it was meant to help people in many different ways. It can be used to condition people to think, act, or behave in ways that are beneficial to them.

If you are subjected to NLP as a form of therapy, it could help you manage your internal state. That means that it can help you control your emotions and the reactions that come with those emotions. As a result, you will be able to act in a more rational and calculated way. It's a form of conditioning that enables you to set aside negative emotions, embrace positive emotions, and to channel your feelings in ways that increase your productivity and utility.

NLP can also help people to stay resourceful during stressful situations. We all experience stress on a day to day basis, and as that stress increases, we tend to become less productive. In extreme cases, we could be paralyzed by stress to the point of inaction. NLP is meant to help people deal with the more difficult aspects of their careers and personal relationships.

NLP helps you to deal with stress by giving you a higher degree of behavioral flexibility when the situation you are dealing with gets a bit difficult. The way we are wired, we tend to get more limited and less flexible as problems become more complex. We are less able to think clearly when exam questions require us to focus. We start babbling when interview questions become more challenging.

If you have ever found yourself in a situation where you only figure out the right solution to a given problem after the event has passed and it's out of your hands, it means you knew the answer all along, but you weren't able to access it at the moment because of the stress. NLP can help keep you from choking at the moment when it counts.

NLP is also used to increase the speed with which a person can learn new information. Whether it's studying at school, some form of vocational training, or learning a new soft skill to improve your career prospects, NLP can go a long way in helping you learn and internalize the core concepts of your new area of study.

NLP can help you to become a more influential member of the teams to which you belong, whether it's at work or in your personal life. NLP can make you a better partner, parent, child, or friend because it makes you more useful and influential to the people in your life.

At work, it can make you a better team player, and better boss, or even a top performer in your department. It could vastly improve your career prospects and make you more suitable for placement in a leadership position.

As we have mentioned, NLP can be used as a tool to model and reproduce excellence in pretty much any field. The two pioneers of NLP (Bandler and Grinder) were once hired by the US Military to help improve their sniper training program.

Now, learning to be a sniper is a fairly complex undertaking. Before the use of NLP, it took the military more than four weeks to trains some of their smartest people to be sharpshooters, and at the end of the month-long program, only 20% of the people were able to pass.

The US Military is one of the most disciplined organizations on the planet, and they have some of the most rigorous programs, and probably the most dedicated servicemen, but no matter how hard they tried, they never could graduate as many snippers as they needed.

Enter the NLP experts. The first thing they did was ask the military to point out who their best snipers were. The military was happy to provide a list of 5 names. In the coming weeks and months, Bandler, Grinder and their team spend a lot of time with the 5 model snippers, observing them and collecting lots of data.

They were trying to find the answer to just one question; "What were these top snippers doing, that set them apart from everyone else?" They looked at what the top snippers were doing with their bodies. They looked at how they perceived their environment. They sought to understand what they were feeling.

They tried to listen to what the model snipers were hearing. They studied how they talked to others and what they told themselves. They reviewed the emotional states that they were in when they took their shots, the mental pictures that they had, etc.

After collecting all that information, Bandler and Grinder were able to come up with a whole new sniper training program that was tailor-made to guarantee excellence. When they were done with designing the program, and when they ran it for the first time, everyone was impressed; it now took only seven days to train the snippers, and they now enjoyed a pass rate that was way over 80%.

The story of the US Military snipper program indicates one crucial thing about NLP; it proves that NLP is highly effective in identifying the key elements in a complex system, or the processes which make a drastic and lasting difference. What's more, all that can be achieved in a few simple steps; all you have to do is model, test, and then reproduce anything you want. Do you want to learn a positive habit? You can find an NLP program that someone has already created, and then follow that program with precision and dedication, and in no time, you will master that habit.

NLP can also be used to alter negative "pathology" behaviors and turn them into positive or useful behaviors. For example, therapists who practice NLP have had some success in treating panic attacks by altering them so that when the stressor is triggered, instead of the patient panicking, they will experience a heightened level of motivation.

These therapists are able to model the behavior behind the panic attack, and then, they proceed to replace the "scary" elements that cause panic attacks with different content that induces intense motivation. People who have panic attacks tend to be imaginative, and they experience intense and vivid visual images. NLP experts can replace those negative visual images with positive ones, so they can channel panic and turn it into motivation.

The Science Behind NLP

To understand the science behind NLP, you have to understand how we process information. Now, there is a lot of information out there in the real world, and scientists have found we can process about 2 million bits of information per second.

In NLP, the real world is called the "territory," and it's where all the information exists. The same scientists also claim that of the 2 million bits of information that we can process, we can only absorb 134 thousand bits per second. When the information hits our brains, we create a "collage" of that information. This is basically a map that gives meaning to what we are perceiving.

We take information in throughout five senses; we see, hear, smell, taste, and feel (touch or sense) the things around us, and it's through these avenues that the information gets into our brains. As we have mentioned, the brain processes 2 million bits and only absorbs 134 thousand bits of information, so, how does this reduction happen?

Well, there are three main ways for the brain to cut down the information. First, the brain will delete some of the information it processes. Second, it will distort the information to make it more manageable. Thirdly, it will generalize some of the information. The brain will decide what information to delete, distort, or generalize, depending on what it thinks is important to you (this could be based on your personality or your past experiences). So, in the end, all the information that the brain collects technically incomplete, and all the perceptions we have are skewed.

Our brains have a library of information that they use to figure out the meaning of the "collages" of information that they collect from the environment. That means our perceptions are subject to our past experiences and the meaning we give to the information we gather, can vary from person to person, even if we are looking at the same thing.

This also means our feelings and our emotional states are subject to the meaning that we give to certain events. The relationship between "meaning" and "emotional state" is very complex. It can go back and forth: the meaning we give to events affects the emotional state we experience as a result of the event, but also, the emotional state we are in affects the meaning we give to things. You see how this can quickly turn into some kind of vicious cycle.

After collecting information, comparing that information to the library in our brains, attaching meaning to the information, and having an emotional reaction to that information, what follows is a physical response based on the information. Again, in this instance, the physical reaction you will have will also be based on the meaning you have attached to the information.

All our experiences, our emotions, perceptions, actions, reactions, memories, etc. are based on the meaning we choose to give them. In other words, we act, feel, or perceive things in a certain way because of the stories we tell ourselves.

Think about it for a second. The things you feel when you are afraid are the same things that you feel when you are excited. The only difference is the meaning you give to the information that's causing the fear or excitement.

When you are fearful, your heart rate will rise, your breathing rate will increase, you may sweat, and you may feel butterflies in the stomach. Those same physical sensations will be manifested when you are excited. Many other emotions mirror each other in the same way. NLP is about altering the meaning one gives to those emotions so that instead of having a negative emotional state or responding with negative action, one becomes more inclined to have a positive emotional state and to take positive actions.

Let's go back to the information we process and absorb. We've mentioned that the brain processes 2 million bits, and absorbs 134 thousand bits, but that kind of downsizing goes a lot further. Of the 134 thousand bits of information the brain absorbs, it can only keep track of about 7 bits of information on average, with a margin of error of plus or minus 2.

This scientific finding has two very important implications. The first is that the vast majority of the information that exists in the environment will go unnoticed by you. The second implication is that we can be able to find whatever information we are looking for if we approach a line of inquiry with certain preconceptions in mind. Both implications are important, but the second one is more crucial, so we need to explain it further.

You may have experienced this at some point in your life. You go home one evening, and your partner or your kid suggests that you should get a dog. Now, this is not something that you have considered in the past, but you have a conversation about it in the evening, and you decide you will think about it and decide in a few days.

Now, the next morning, you drive to work, and the first thing you notice as you pull off the driveway is a neighbor's dog running down the street. As you keep on driving, you see several dogs on the side of the road. A few miles along the highway, you notice there is a dog park along your regular route, which for some reason, you hadn't seen before. You drive into town, and you spot a pet food store. As you walk into your office, you notice, for the first time in months or years, that a few of your colleagues have pictures of their dogs on their desks.

What's going on here? It's not like this information didn't exist in your environment all this time. The reason you are noticing things related to dogs is that you are paying attention to those things. Your partner's or child's suggestion to get a dog is at the back of your mind, so when you take in information from the environment, and your brain runs that information through its library, then the dog-related information pops up first in your brain's "search results."

This explains why, when you want something at some level, you start to feel as though "the universe" or "God" is sending you a sign. In reality, the brain is just tracking certain information that is at the back of your mind. The brain has decided to "tune in" to that information because it thinks the information is relevant to you at that particular time.

So, as you can see, the brain can choose which information to tune into, and which information to exclude from your conscious perception. NLP is not really about changing the information that is available to a person. Instead, it's about controlling which information the person's brain ends up prioritizing.

In the modern practice of NLP, people can use various tricks and techniques to alter their own perceptions, or the perceptions of others, in order to control their own feelings or behavior (or those of other people).

You can ask a therapist or someone who is well versed in NLP to help you improve certain aspects of your life using NLP techniques. You can learn NLP techniques and use them to improve your own life. Finally, you can learn NLP techniques and use them to influence or control the behaviors of others.

Chapter 6: Dark NLP Techniques

We've mentioned several times in the previous chapter that when NLP was originally conceived, it was meant to help people. However, pretty much all the NLP techniques that have been developed over the decades can be co-opted by people withmalicious intentions, who can use them to manipulate others for their own benefit.

Dark NLP techniques are those techniques used to control others with the aim of taking advantage of them or causing them harm. To that end, any NLP technique can be considered as a dark technique if it falls into the wrong hands. Anyone with an understanding of NLP techniques can program others in a way that is detrimental to them.

Technically, it can be argued that we all use NLP to control the people around us in one way or another without even realizing it. We don't always do it out of malice, but it occurs naturally to some extent. Let's say you meet someone, and you smile at them. That will affect their emotional state; they'll have a warm feeling inside, and they may smile back at you.

Now, suppose you are having a conversation with someone, and whenever they say something pleasant, you smile at them. Now, in the course of the conversation, they bring up a topic you find unpleasant. The smile on your face vanishes, and it's replaced with a scowl. The other person reads your body language and decides to drop that topic and move on to something else. When they get started on a different topic, you start smiling again. You may not be schooled in the art of NLP, but what's happened here is you have used a very simple NLP technique to get someone to do what you want; you have manipulated someone!

Now, the NLP techniques manipulators use to influence people are more complex than a smile, but they work the same way. They condition the other person to alter their behavior at a subconscious level. Dark NLP practitioners learn NLP techniques the same way everyone else does, but after mastering the NLP skills, they decide to "use their powers for evil."

Let's talk about the most common Dark NLP techniques.

Anchoring

An anchor is a stimulus that produces a certain emotional reaction in you. To understand anchoring, think about any song that you like. Preferably one you heard a long time ago, and you haven't heard in a while. Supposing you are driving along the highway in your car, and then suddenly, that song comes on the radio; what are you going to feel?

Maybe you will be reminded of the first time you heard the song and the memories and emotions associated with that one instance. Maybe you will think about the period when that song was popular, when you were much younger, or when things in your life were much simpler. Even if you don't remember the details of whatever issues you were dealing with when you first heard the song, the emotions you felt back then will surge in you.

There is a simple explanation here; because you were feeling certain emotions at the time you heard the song, your subconscious mind linked the songs to the feelings, so when you hear the song once again after so many years, your brain is triggered to feel the same way it did back then. In other words, the song is an anchor to the feelings, and it has the ability to pull you back to the place you were all those years ago.

Ivan Pavlov is famous for the conditioning experiments that he conducted on dogs. He would ring a bell before feeding his dogs. After some time, the dogs came to associate the ringing sound with food, so that when they heard the bell, they would start to salivate. As humans, we claim to be smarter than all other life forms, but we too can be conditioned in the same way. It is possible to manipulate someone by introducing an anchor into their subconscious mind, and then triggering thatanchor when you want them to do certain things or to feel certain emotions.

Well-meaning therapists and NLP practitioners use anchoring to help people deal with emotional turbulence. For example, can tap into your subconscious and bring forth good memories from your past, then anchor those memories to something you or they can control. They can hypnotize you in such a way that when they touch your shoulder, some of your good memories come flashing back into your mind.

People can hire NLP therapists to help them create powerful resource states, which they can trigger when they need to. In such cases, anchoring requires four key elements.

First, the therapists would put the client in a pure and strong resource state (where they feel happy, highly motivated, and not at all emotionally conflicted).

The second thing the therapist has to do is ensure the emotional state is very intense. The more intense the state, the stronger the anchor is going to be, so therapists will time the anchor in such a way that it's introduced at the moment when the emotional state is about to peak, and it's maintained up to the point when the state is starting to decline.

The third element that NLP therapists consider is the uniqueness of the stimulus that is used to anchor the person. It can't be something the person experiences on a daily basis. If the stimulus is experienced regularly, the brain won't be able to link it exclusively to a specific emotional state.

Finally, the stimulus has to be easily replicable. It has to be something you can easily trigger whenever you need to.

Manipulative people, use anchoring to control other people so that they can take advantage of them or gain the upper hand over them. Remember, all they have to do is condition you so you recall a certain memory or you experience a certain change in your state in response to a specific stimulus which they can trigger whenever they need to. When you perceive the stimulus in question, you will reflexively respond in the way they have conditioned you to.

The stimulus used to anchor a person can be pretty much anything, and it often engages one or more of your five senses. The stimulus could be a touch on your shoulder, a certain word used in conversation, a certain image introduced within your field of vision, etc. Manipulative people are more likely to use a neutral stimulus, one that will escape your conscious awareness.

Remember, anchoring can be used to make recall good or bad memories, and it can be used to make you feel either positive or negative emotions, so the manipulative person will use anchoring to condition you however they like, and in whichever way it serves their best interests.

If, for example, it's a colleague who thinks of you as his nemesis—he could use anchoring to bring forth bad memories and negative emotions so as to sabotage you. If you are dating a person who is manipulative and controlling, he may use anchoring to make you feel positive emotions towards him.

The anchoring done by hypnotherapists in controlled sessions is slightly different from the kind done by manipulative people out there in the real world. While a hypnotherapist may try to tap into your memories in order to anchor you, a manipulative person (one that is in your life) will try to be subtle. He may try to introduce an anchor into your subconscious mind over a long period of time. Remember, just like Ivan Pavlov's dogs, the more often the anchoring stimulus is associated with certain memories or emotional states, the more it sticks, and the better it works.

Here is a simple pop-culture example that can help you better understand how the concept of anchoring works. In one episode of the CBS sitcom *How I Met Your Mother*, one character named Barney uses anchoring to condition his friend Marshall to act in a very specific way in the future. Every time Marshall suggests they go to a certain restaurant, Barney would sneeze, and Marshall would say, "Bless you."

After this happens many times over, it gets to a point where things start working the other way around. Whenever Barney would sneeze, his friend would immediately have a craving for Japanese food. Now, this is a fictional example that is played out for comic reasons, but it perfectly illustrates how anchoring could be used to condition someone in the real world; a stimulus (the sound of a sneeze in this case) is used to create a desire (a craving for a certain type of food).

Mirroring

Mirroring is a natural behavior people use to create rapport between each other in social settings. When two people are getting along with each other in a conversation or any other social situation, they tend to subconsciously mirror each other's emotions, facial expressions, posture, hand placement, etc. In psychology, we understand that mirroring is a sign of harmony between two people and that those people trust each other on some subconscious level.

Like we've mentioned, dark NLP techniques work the same way that ordinary NLP techniques do, the only difference being the intention of the person using them. People mirror each other subconsciously with no ill intent. Some people can consciously mirror others because they are trying to influence them, but they do it with pure intentions.

There are well developed NLP techniques that teach people how to mirror others in order to improve their relationships and to improve their own emotional intelligence.

Manipulators, however, consciously mirror others because they want to trick them into believing on a subconscious level that there is a connection between them; the ultimate goal here is to exploit the rapport it created as a result of the mirroring.

The first, and perhaps the easiest mirroring technique that you can learn is the one that involves copying other people's outward cues. The quickest way to create a rapport between you and someone else is to match their outward physiology.

At this point, it's important to note that mirroring is not the same thing as copying or mimicking someone. While mimicking is obvious and instant, mirroring is subtle, and when properly done, it can bypass the other person's conscious mind and only register in their subconscious.

Mimicking, on the other hand, will be instantly noticed by the other person, and instead of creating or establishing a rapport, it will only serve to annoy the other person, and that will be counterproductive.

When you mirror someone's physiology, you will subtly observe their body language, and try to match their legs, hands, arm position, torso, or even the tilt of their head.

You can also mirror people's posture; if they are sitting upright, or in a slumped position, if they are leaning to left or to the right, etc.

It's also possible to mirror people's gestures. To do this accurately, you have to observe them for a considerable amount of time. If you are close enough to a person, you can mirror their breathing rate. If you are walking next to the person, you can mirror their pace.

When conversing with a person, you can mirror their voice; you can adjust your own voice to match their pitch, tone, volume, and even the speed at which they are talking.

It's also possible to mirror someone's language. When you pay attention to the way a person speaks, you will realize that they tend to use certain keywords and phrases. When they talk about things they are passionate about or things important to them, they tend to put emphasis on certain words. You can learn these words, and you can start feeding them back to the person in order to create a rapport with them.

You can also mirror a person's eye-related cues. There are people whose eyes water and glisten when they are passionate about certain topics of conversation. There are those who look in certain directions when they are trying to recall facts, or they adjust their eyebrows in certain ways when they are feeling certain emotions.

You can observe such people for some time and then mirror their eye-related cues. The point is to make them see themselves in you, just as they would in an actual mirror. It indicates to them that you understand how they are feeling. We all tend to like people who share certain traits with us, and mirroring someone's eye cues indicates to them you are just like them.

Mirroring can go far beyond the outward cues. Both well-meaning NLP practitioners and manipulative people are able to mirror the internal personality traits of others.

When you spend time with a person, it's possible to figure out if they value things like honesty, politeness, and respect. Once you figure out their values, you can mirror them, to the point of convincing them that you actually share those values.

It's also possible to mirror a person's belief structures. You can find out what the person believes and then indicate to them in a subtle way that you share those beliefs.

The more sophisticated manipulators and dark NLP practitioners are able to mirror other people's habitual thinking patterns. They can spend time with a person and figure out if they are optimists or pessimists, and they can learn a lot of details about their outlook and general attitudes. After that, they are able to mirror the other person's thinking patterns by dropping hints that indicate that they share those patterns.

For manipulators, the end goal of mirroring it to get to control the other person. To that end, they will mirror the person to the point wherethey can set the pace for them, and later, they can take the lead over their lives. When you mirror a person, you are telling their subconscious minds that the two of you are on the same page and you see eye to eye on certain issues.

They get the sense you are with them, and they let lower their guard and let you in. They allow you to occupy the same open and connective space with them, and once you are at that point, you gain the power to impact their lives. At this point, manipulative people could use other NLP techniques, or general manipulation techniques to further their personal agendas.

Calibration

You might remember your science teacher talking about calibration in the context of measurements. In NLP, calibration is about being able to measure or gauge a person's emotional state with precision. You probably already know you can tell a lot about what a person is thinking or feeling at any given time just by paying attention to their verbal and nonverbal cues (including body language, eyes, breathing patterns, etc.).

Calibration in NLP takes things further than that. It's not just about spotting a scowl on someone's face; it's about paying keen attention to the subtlest of clues. Calibration is about noticing and measuring all the changes in a person during an ongoing interaction. That person could be you, or it could be someone else.

If you are using NLP as a self-improvement tool, you will have to calibrate yourself so you learn to take notice when you are shifting from one emotional state to another.

Manipulative people use calibration to read people so they can take advantage of the shifts in their emotional states, or so they can plant anchors and use them to control those shifts themselves.

For calibration to work, you have to establish a standard. Just like any other form of measurement you can think of, calibration only works when there is a frame of reference to which you can compare whatever emotion states you are observing in a person. That means that for you to properly calibrate someone, you have to spend a lot of time observing them in ordinary situations and seeing how they transition between different emotional states.

The observable changes include changes in posture, voice, facial cues, and the use of gestures. However, you have to understand that everyone has different mannerisms and different tendencies, so you can't calibrate a person based on generalized assumptions.

You must start with a baseline read of the person you are calibrating. After you have a baseline, you can consider any deviation from that baseline to be a noteworthy change, and you can then try to figure out what that change means to that particular person.

You have to use your sensory acuity when you are establishing a person's baseline so that you can calibrate them. In fact, in most NLP literature, calibration is considered to be a component of sensory equity. Sensory acuity refers to that innate ability in all of us to read others.

Even though we all have it to some extent, it's a skill that can be sharpened with deliberate practice. Sensory acuity can be used to assess minor detail in anyone you observe. When you look at someone's eyes during an interaction, you can tell whether or not their pupils are dilated. If you pay attention to the person's skin tone, you might be able to notice minor changes in muscle tension in their face, or when they shift to certain emotional states, blood could rush into their faces and make their cheeks red.

You can take note of a person's facial symmetry because when some people experience certain emotions, they tend to distort their faces in one direction or another. You also have to observe the subject's lip sizes and orientation so if a change occurs in the mouth area, you can properly calibrate it.

More experienced NLP practitioners have the sensory acuity to observe things like changes in a person's pulse, and they can even detect changes in breathing from a considerable distance. If the person performing the calibration is a well-meaning practitioner of NLP, he may engage you in a casual conversation at first so that he can take his time to observe your baseline behavior. A malicious or manipulative person, on the other hand, will try to observe your baseline in a subtle way.

After establishing a proper baseline, manipulative people will keep observing their targets to see if they can decipher any emotions based on behavioral patterns. Behavioral patterns can be clear indicators of emotions, especially when they are analyzed in specific contexts.

For example, a person who is talking about a sad experience may show the following behavioral patterns; the voice may be softer than the baseline, the volume may be lower than usual, they may stare at the floor, they may talk at a slow pace, and their legs may shake a bit. When a person is describing a happy memory, they may speak at a higher volume, and at a faster pace, they may maintain eye contact or look up, and they may smile broadly. When NLP manipulators spend time with someone, they notice all the behavioral patterns that the person manifests when they are happy, sad, excited, fearful, anxious, etc. At this point, they can figure out ways to use other NLP techniques such as anchoring or mirroring to manipulate the person, or they can use direct manipulation techniques.

For instance, if a manipulative colleague has learned all your behavioral patterns, then one day, he notices that you are showing patterns that indicate anxiety when talking about an upcoming project presentation, he can use that against you by feeding your anxiety so as to grow it further and to sabotage you.

Mapping Across

This is an NLP technique that makes use of modalities and sub-modalities. The way it works is that the sub-modalities under a particular modality can be taken and then implanted under a different modality so as to alter a person's beliefs about the second modality. If all this sounds too technical, don't worry, we'll break down the concept and use examples to explain how it works. Anyone can benefit from this NLP technique. You can learn it and use it on yourself, or you can hire an NLP expert to use the technique on you. Just like with all other NLP techniques, manipulative people can also co-opt the practice of mapping across and use it to condition people in ways that harm the people and benefit the manipulators. To understand how the concept of mapping across works, think of something that you have to do on a regular basis, but you dislike doing. Maybe you hate doing certain chores at home or handling giant stacks of paperwork at school. Now, think of something that you enjoy doing. Maybe you love to go out dancing, or you have fun hanging out at a certain bar. Mapping across involves transferring the elements from one state and putting them into another state.

As we have mentioned, the resource state refers to the state where you are happy and productive. The aim of mapping (when it's done for self-improvement purposes) is to replicate the resource state in situations where you aren't as resourceful.

So, in our example above, the resource state is the one where you enjoy dancing, and the sub-modalities are the positive emotions and mental pictures you experience, and the mental energy you have when you are in that state. What needs to be done is to transfer those sub-modalities so you start associating the chores you hate with the positive emotions and the high levels of energy you have when you are dancing. That may seem simple, but mapping across is a fairly complex process. This process is sometimes referred to as overlapping. The first step in the process is to identify the emotional state or the negative experience which you wish to change. If you are doing it on yourself, you have to make sure you are fully associated with that particular state at the moment.

Trained NLP experts can guide you through a set of steps that can help you feel as though you are re-experiencing the whole process all over again like it's some sort of vivid dream that brings the memories to the surface. If you are dealing with a hypnotist, he may ask you to paint a mental picture of that experience; to see it as vividly as you can in your head, and to give it a color, shape, size, and many other physical attributes. As you mention the attributes you associate with that experience, the person doing the mapping will take note of those attributes and try to figure out which ones to use as sub-modalities. The next step involves finding a different experience, one that is somewhat similar to the one you would like to change. It's crucial that this experience should have a relatively similar structure to the one you are looking to change.

Let's take the example of a person who eats a lot of candy bars. This person recognizes that addiction to candy is a problem because it's detrimental to his health. He goes to an NLP practitioner for help. The NLP practitioner assesses the situation, and it's clear to him what needs to change. He picks the mental image of the client holding an unwrapped candy bar in the first step of the mapping-across process. After talking to the client for a while, he realizes the client has a dog for a pet. Now, he figures out he could use the mental image of the client picking up her dog's excrement as an experience that has general similarities to the first experience. At this point, we have two clear experiences: experience 1 (candy bar in hand) and experience 2 (dog excrement in hand).

Now, the third step of the mapping across process involves comparing these two experiences to figure out the differences in sub-modalities. As long as the two experiences have comparable structures, the sub-modalities that are similar are not relevant to the mapping across process (since they are the same either way, they are of no use to the NLP practitioner). Usually, there won't be too many differences between the experiences. In fact, if there are several usable experiences, the NLP expert will pick the one closest to the problematic one.

Of the two experiences to be cross-mapped, one may be 'associated' (large, vivid, and colorful), and the other may be 'dissociated' (vague, small, and in black-and-white). One may be perceived by the client as a colorful 3D video with clear sounds, while the other could be seen as a tiny picture with neutral colors. The fourth step of cross-mapping involves altering one of the elements in experience 1 (one of the different sub-modalities) with the corresponding element in experience 2. The idea here is that after comparing two things, one you like to do and one you don't, and after distilling it down and identifying the core differences, you can make someone (or yourself) start liking what she used to dislike by replacing an undesirable element with a desirable element, and you can make her dislike what she used to like by replacing a desirable element with an undesirable one.

In the example of the candy bar and the dog excrement, you can replace the sweet smell of the candy with the foul smell of dog excrement, and this will make the candy bar less desirable for the person who needs to cut down.

Chapter 7: How to Understand People

Psychology is defined as the scientific study of the human mind and its functions. In terms of the functions of the mind, psychology focuses mostly on those that relate to human behavior. For you to understand people, you have to have a basic understanding of psychology. As a point of caution, though, you have to remember not to put too much stock in psychology—in as much as it's a science, it's not an exact science.

In exact sciences (like physics), standardized formulas and theories are universally applicable. However, in psychology, even if there is a theory that is backed by extensive scientific evidence, you still have to make a lot of inferences. That is because of one fundamental fact: people are different.

If you want to understand people, the first thing you need to learn is that there can't be a general formula that explains human behavior. You can try to understand people, and you can tell with a high degree of accuracy what their thoughts, emotions, and motivations are, but you cannot generalize. You have to make your assessments on a case by case basis.

So, why is it so important to understand people? Well, in this book, we are looking at techniques that you can use to influence people on a subconscious level, and unless you understand how the human mind works, you will be flying blind. More important than that, you too are human; understanding people, in general, will help you understand yourself better. You aim to understand people and not to judge them, so you should avoid making assumptions about them. You will never be able to understand people if you make snap judgments about them. Supposing you meet someone and your first impression is that she is mean and unfriendly. If you are quick to judge, you will assume that's just who she is, but if you take time to understand her, you may discover she is shy or uncomfortable with strangers. Try to keep an open mind about people, because many of them are deeper than their first impressions.

Understanding People's Motivations

In as much as Psychology is complex, and human behavior tends to vary immensely, there is a common thread that can help you to understand people in general, and that is human motivation. No matter where they are in the world, no matter what paths they take in life, and no matter how they are perceived by the societies they live in, humans tend to have similar motivations, and figuring out what those motivations are, is the key to figuring out ways to influence those people using subconscious means.

Motivations are the things that drive people to do certain things, and some of them are innate in all of us. In as much as people are different, they want the same things out of life. To illustrate this, let's take the example of 2 teenage boys. One grows up in an upscale suburb, and the other one grows up on the "wrong side of the tracks." The first boy works hard through high school and joins a prestigious university, where he trains to be a doctor. The second boy drops out of high school, joins a gang, and tries to work his way to the top of the gang pyramid. There two people may be different in every imaginable way, but if you distill things down, you will find that they have similar motivations.

Here are the motivations the two boys share:

- They both yearn for self-actualization. In as much as their approaches are different, both boys have a desire to be wealthy, they feel they have the capacity to actualize that goal, and they are all working to accomplish their goals.

- They are motivated by a need for self-protection. Both boys are hoping for safety and security. They want a steady income (job security), and they want to be safe from harm. In his mind, the boy who joins the gang believes that his membership in the gang will make him appear though, and that will keep him safe.

- Both boys are motivated by a need for love and belonging. The boy who goes to a great school wants to be part of an elite group of intellectuals, and the boy who joins the gang may think of the other gang members as his family.

- Both boys are looking for status or are lookingto be held in high esteem. The boy who goes to a great college wants to be seen as smart and a member of an elite group. The boy who joins a gang wants to have "street credit" (a reputation for toughness).

- Both boys want to acquire and retain a mate. The boy who goes to college will flaunt his intelligence in order to get a suitable mate. The boy who joins a gang will leverage his "street credit" to attract a suitable mate.

When you look at it that way, you realize that people can be easy to figure out from a motivational standpoint. However, motivation is just the tip of the iceberg; you still have to assess their emotions and behavior and try to figure out their thoughts.

How to Observe People

To understand people, you have to be an astute observer of human behavior. When you observe people, you are able to collect the data you need in order to analyze it and predict their emotional and behavioral tendencies. Observing people is a skill you have to develop over time with practice. The first thing you need to do is to slow down a bit; with the hustle and bustle of everyday life, we all learn to be in a hurry, and we don't pay attention to others. If you want to be good at observing people, you have to take your time to make eye contact with people, to participate in small talk, to truly listen to what people are saying, to pay attention to people's body language, posture, and gestures, and to notice the clothes they are wearing.

You have to start with the people in your vicinity, and that means your family members and your friends. If you have a habit of staring at your phone or your tablet on the breakfast table, checking your email while you are half-listening to your partner's or your child's stories, it's time to put an end to that. Being a good listener is a crucial part of being a good observer, so look directly at whoever you are talking to and try to engage with them. When you say "hello" to colleagues along the corridor, stop, look them in the eye, and extend your hand in greeting.

When you are taking public transportation with total strangers, practice being observant. You can make a fun game out of it. Imagine you are Sherlock Holmes. Look at the strangers one by one, and try to create stories about who they are and what they are up to, based on the things you observe about them.

To observe people, you also need to get out of your own head. We are all constantly preoccupied with our own obsessions (whether it is thoughts, insecurities, or desires that we have) and that is a constant source of distraction that keeps us from truly paying attention to the verbal and nonverbal cues of others. It's okay to have an inner life, but being observant means taking in the world around you, and concentrating on other people. Getting out of your own head won't be easy because your thought patterns are stored in well-established neural networks in your brain, but with concerted effort, you can change them. Just try to be more aware of your own thoughts instead of letting them run on autopilot; this will help you to focus on the people you are observing consciously. Finally, as you observe people, you need to learn to do it in a subtle way. Scientists have long observed that the very act of observing a phenomenon can actually change it, and the same thing applies to humans. If you stare at someone in an attempt to observe his/her cues, he/she will get self-conscious and will, therefore, change his/her behavior, and you won't get an accurate read.

Chapter 8: Psychoanalyzing People

You can't talk about psychoanalysis without talking about Sigmund Freud—he is the father of psychoanalysis. He was an Austrian doctor who believed people could be cured if their unconscious thoughts and motivation could be consciously understood. According to him, if people could consciously articulate why the act and felt the way they did, maybe they'd be able to get their mental and emotional issues under control.

Since Freud's time, psychoanalysis has evolved around the world, and in as much as it's still used in controlled clinical settings, anyone with a basic understanding of how it works has the ability to use it to his advantage—anyone can psychologically analyze others with the end goal of influencing them. In this chapter, we look at techniques you can use to psychoanalyze the people in your life.

Distinguishing Between Introverts and Extroverts

One way to figure people out is by seeking to understand whether they are introverts or extroverts. Knowing this alone can help you make plenty of quick judgments about pretty much anyone. Introverts are people who draw their energy from within, which means that they feel more energized when they are alone or in laid back situations.

Extroverts, on the other hand, draw their mental energy from without, so they are more energized when they are in social situations. If you want to psychoanalyze someone, figuring out which category they fall under should be one of the first things you do.

Spotting an Introvert

If you want to tell if someone is an introvert, you have to observe them during social situations. Introverts will show up to social situations when they are required to, or when they have company, but few of them will go out of the way to attend every optional gathering. Hence, if your colleague doesn't show up for office parties or after work drinks, that could be a sign he is an introvert (of course, there is always the chance he prefers handing out elsewhere). When introverts do show up for social functions, they will be able to mingle and interact with other people, but their behavior will be noticeably different from the extroverts. For starters, they will be more inclined to spend time on the sidelines, so they certainly won't be the "life of the party." If the person you want to analyze tends to spend time on the edges of the room, to talk to just a few people, and she seems to be deeply focused on the conversation she is having, there is a high probability she is introverted.

If the person you are analyzing seems to like spending time out in nature, there is a high probability that he/she is introverted. For introverts, time out in nature is an escape from the hustle and bustle of work or everyday life. If a colleague likes to go fishing or hunting, or if he has an odd hobby like birdwatching, he might be an introvert. Introverts will go out of their way to avoid being the center of attention. In meetings, they'll introduce themselves in a very formal and professional manner. During presentations, they will stick with the facts, and they'll make things brief and efficient.

Introverts also tend to be better at communicating through writing than speaking their thoughts out loud, so, if your boss is more likely to send out memos that call for impromptu meetings, he could be introverted. Introverts will try to avoid small-talk as much as possible, or they'll keep it to a minimum. They are less likely to "hang by the water cooler" at work, or to tell jokes in professional settings.

You might also be dealing with an introvert: If the person you are analyzing seems a bit too intense, if he tends to notice the kinds of details most other people miss, if he seems to be able to concentrate on his work for longer periods of time than the average person, if he strikes you as a good listener, and if he doesn't seem to have too many friends.

Spotting an Extrovert

Extroverts should be easier to spot than introverts. For starters, they love to talk, so you will always notice them. They talk to everyone; they have hearty conversations with friends, family, and colleagues; they'll strike up a conversation with a total stranger, and in no time, they will be chatting like old friends. Extroverts tend to have very many friends, both in real life and on social media. Making friends comes easy to them, and unlike introverts, they never have to overthink things in social situations.

When extroverts are in social gatherings, they feel energized, and they get inspired. They are always the ones calling their friends up and coming up with plans to go out. In the office, they are the ones who invite everyone to happy hour, and they take part in extracurricular activities (like playing for the office softball team). When interpersonal conflicts arise, extroverts will want to discuss the problems out loud and solve them instantly (introverts, on the other hand, might avoid addressing problems that could result in any form of confrontation). When other people talk about extroverts, they often describe them as friendly and approachable. When you meet them, they'll strike you as open, and you will feel like it's really easy to get to know them.

Psychoanalysis Based on People's Motivations

As you may have learned in the previous chapter, if you know the motivations and the wants of the people around you, then you understand them well enough to be able to influence them. Psychology and psychoanalysis are very vast fields, and it will be futile to try to dip into the highly technical aspects of those fields in this book. The point of this is to distill information into comprehensible and actionable chunks regular people can start using immediately.

So, if you want to psychoanalyze your friends, family, coworkers, and enemies, we will show you have to understand their motives, and how those motives predict their behaviors, decision making, and their weaknesses.

When you can psychoanalyze people and understand them, you will be able to steer clear of any conflicts with them. You will be able to control all your interactions in such a way that you get the maximum benefit from them. You will be able to condition people so they can help you achieve your goals. Many people fail to get along with others and they waste a lot of their time complaining about others, trying to modify their behavior, and feeling frustrated, because they make one key error in judgment:

they expect everyone else to be just like them, to share their values and their thought processes, and to act in ways that they consider to be rational. But the fact is that everyone is different. Even identical twins raised by the same parents with the same values, end up having different world views.

You have to start with the premise that everyone has their own inner world and their own perspectives. Since age 3, we are all aware of the fact people have different information available to them because they have different experiences from us, but even then, we find it really hard to conceive of the fact that people could perceive reality in a different way from us. That is the biggest hurdle you'll have to overcome when you psychoanalyze people; the tendency to look at their world through your own perspective instead of theirs. When you want to psychoanalyses someone, you have to stop trying to explain them in terms of your own emotions, thought patterns, assumptions, and experiences. Remember, in the previous chapter; we talked about two boys who had similar motivations; one went to an elite university, and the other joined a street gang. If the boy who went to the fancy school ever met the one who was in a gang, he would most likely apply his own world view and make a quick judgment that his counterpart was just a "common criminal."

That kind of stereotypical thinking is natural (and it even serves a valid evolutionary function because it can help one perceive danger and react immediately), but if you want to be good a psychoanalyzing people, you have to be consciously aware of your own prejudices, and you have to adjust for those prejudices in your final assessment of the person you are analyzing.

As we've said, you need to understand your subjects' motivations, but that in itself is a complex challenge. We talked in the previous chapter about some motivations that are common in almost everyone, but for the purposes of psychoanalysis, those universal motivations are too general to yield any kind of actionable information. They are manifested in so many iterations; psychologists have been able to identify more than 700 different human motivations. The other part of the challenge when you are trying to pinpoint a person's exact motivations is that you can't just walk up to them and ask them. Most of the time, asking about a person's motivations will be perceived as a sign of aggression.

Even in the few instances where the person may be open to offering you a straight answer, you may end up discovering that either the person doesn't know his/her motivations, or he/she is actually mistaken about them. A person may think he is motivated by a need to succeed, but it could turn out that he is mistaken, and deep within, he is really motivated by a need to fill an emotional wound. In psychoanalysis, you have to look deep to tell the difference between cause and effect. You may think something is a cause (a core motivation), but it turns out to be an effect (a secondary motivation that is predicated upon something more primal).

Psychoanalysis is like peeling an onion. You have to tear someone down layer by layer until you get to who they are at the core. In practice, you will have to start from the most outward information available to you, and you will have to keep augmenting that information until you get to most basic motives that drive that person; a motive is only considered to be basic if it can't be broken down much further. For any person you analyze, their basic motivation is the answer to the question, "What does he/she really want?"

Here are the steps that you should take when you are psychoanalyzing a person (if you have professional training in psychology, you may be aware of other more complex processes, but this one is designed to be as simple and straight forward as possible so that anyone can use it). The steps we will discuss are about how you can collect useful information upon which you can base your analysis.

Step 1: Background

At this stage, you will start by exchanging general information with the person that you are analyzing. You will have small-talk with the person, and you will try to elicit as much personal information about them as you possibly can. Remember, you are doing this covertly, so avoid coming across as too aggressive.

When you gather this information, don't think too much of it; some of it may be valuable later in the process, but some of it may just be junk. Try to get the person's history; an individual's history is important because it helps you when you want to test different theories about their actual motives. Here, you might find out when the person was born, what their childhood was like, what they studied in college (if they did go to college), what they do for a living, how long they've been on the job, etc.

Step 2: Assess Appearance

Our outward appearance is the most visible manifestation of who we are and what motivates us. The way we choose to present ourselves to the world speaks volumes about the mental processes that occur deep in our subconscious minds. You should assess the person's appearance because it gives a reflection of who the person is inside.

However, as a point of caution, you shouldn't jump to conclusions about a person's motivations based on the way they appear. Some people like to put on "masks" to hide their motivations. An overly ambitious person might tone down the way he dresses to seem less threatening to the people around him. When you assess a person's appearance, you can make a note of their hairstyle and color, their level of physical fitness (their general physique), the clothes they are wearing, the accessories they have on, their shoes, their makeup, etc.

Step 3: Assess Behavior

Behavior is similar to a person's appearance in the sense that it's a good indicator of a person's basic nature. However, as a tool for psychoanalysis, it's much more potent because while someone can modify their looks, it is exponentially more difficult for them to modify their behavior. Even the most deceptive people are unable to hide their body language signals for long. They may try to appear composed when they meet you for the first time, but they'll resort to being their real selves once the ice is broken.

There are literary thousands of possible behavioral traits, and after spending a little time with someone, you will pick up on their more dominant behavioral traits.

Take note of how loudly or softly, the person talks, and if he/she tends to interrupt others during conversations. If it's a woman, what she does with her hair as she talks can be quite revealing. You can get a general sense of their temper. Also, pay attention to what the person does with his/her hands. You may be able to gauge the person's level of agreeableness, whether they are patient or impatient, whether they like to work alone or in teams, how good of a listener they are, and how they walk. The bottom line is if you notice anything about the person that sets him/her apart from most other people, it's worth taking note.

Step 4: Assessing the Person's Words

As you talk to the person, pay attention to the kinds of words they choose to use. We all have access to the same set of words, but you will be able to notice if a person is particularly fond of certain words and expressions. If you hear a person use words that are uncommon, it could be an expression of their personality. Psychologists have long understood that people tend to develop certain "pet words," which reflect their world view and their personalities. A person's language skills can also reveal a lot to you. Good vocabulary and advanced language skills can be a sign of intelligence. Pretentious words, on the other hand, can be a sign of insecurity (the person goes out of his way to try to get others to think he is smart).

Step 5: Assess the Person's Preferred Topics of Conversation

As you casually converse with the person that you want to psychoanalyze, let the conversation take its natural course, and give him/her the leeway to steer the conversation however they like. When a person talks openly and has control over the course of the conversation, he/she will naturally bring up topics about which he/she is passionate. People tend to voice whatever is at the back of their minds without realizing it. If you are dealing with someone who is consumed by vengeance, for instance, he/she is more likely to spend a lot of time obsessing over the people who have wronged him/her, and he/she may even openly share some revenge fantasies with you. Even when you are talking about general interests, try to figure out what topics the person is drawn towards. For example, you can infer a lot about a person's motivations if they tell you they are interested in art, economics, sciences, investment, sports, etc.

Step 6: Assess the Person's Likes

People's likes are perhaps the most direct clues to their motivations. Likes tend to link to motives in a very straightforward way. You don't have to connect too many dots to get to what drives a person to like a certain thing. If a person likes to study, then he is motivated by a need for self-actualization (read hard, get a good job, be somebody important). When someone says they like to run, they want to be fit, and fitness is about confidence and respect. When different likes are combined together, you might find a pattern that explains the person's motivation in a more comprehensive way.

Step 7: Assess the Things the Person Avoids

Avoidance is something that happens on a subconscious level. It's easy to figure out the things that a person seeks out, but the things that he avoids can easily go unnoticed unless you are there to witness his reactions to those things. You need to have a particularly keen eye to tell what it is that a person is trying to avoid. Just like the things a person likes, the things he avoids can indicate his true nature. Under the right circumstances, you might be able to tell if a person tends to avoid conflict if he avoids conversations, he thinks are uncomfortable or boring, if he tends to avoid commitment if he tries to stay away from drunks, if he avoids noisy or chaotic places, etc.

Step 8: Assess How the Person Views Himself

When you psychoanalyze someone, you are essentially trying to build a model of who that person is. It is, therefore, a matter of keen interest for you to find out how that person views himself. When you assess a person's self-view, you get to understand what his needs are. People have an uncanny ability to deceive and to delude themselves, into thinking that they already are who they aspire to be. That means if you take note of a person's self-view, you can realize what his aspirations are, and then you can work backward to uncover the motive behind the aspiration. Since you have already assessed the person's behavior, when you seek to understand how he views himself, you can pay attention to how he rationalizes his behavior. You can elicit this information by asking the person directly.

The Key to Psychoanalyzing People: Interpreting Motives and Desires

When you are done with the 8 steps, you will have with you a trove of raw information about the person you want to psychoanalyze—and it is now time to make sense of all that information.

There are many ways to group and to assess people's motives, but for our purposes, we will use the 16 Basic Desires Theory, which was conceptualized by Steven Reiss. Reiss, a professor of psychology and psychiatry, spent his career studying human motivation, and he came up with 16 different "needs" that exist in all people to varying degrees. According to him, these are "basic desires" that motivate people, and drive them to act in certain ways or to hold certain beliefs. Those drives are:

- ACCEPTANCE (the need to be appreciated)

- CURIOSITY (the need to acquire knowledge)

- EATING (the need for sustenance)

- FAMILY (the need to care for one's children)

- HONOR (the need to adhere to customary values, the loyalty to tribe, family, clan, one's parents)

- IDEALISM (need for fairness and justice)

- INDEPENDENCE (need to rely on oneself, to be distinct from others)

- ORDER (need to exist in environments that are well prepared and established in a conventional sense)

- PHYSICAL ACTIVITY (need to exercise one's body)

- POWER (need to have control over one's will)

- ROMANCE (need for sex or mating)

- SAVING (need to collect things)

- SOCIAL CONTACT (need to have relationships with others)

- TRANQUILITY (need for security and protection)

- VENGEANCE (need to confront and strike back against "deserving" people)

You can look at the information you have collected, and try to figure out which of the person's motivations are the most dominant. Go through each of the 8 steps that we have talked about, and for each quality, you have observed, find out which motivation they represent.

For example, if the person went to a great college and chose a challenging major, it means that he is motivated by curiosity. If the person is physically fit, he is motivated by physical exercise; if the person seems to put a lot of work into his/her appearance, romance could be a dominant motivation. If the person has started her own business and she works alone, she could be motivated by independence. If the person pays attention to details and is well organized, she could be motivated by a need for order. Don't just focus on the motives for which people rate highly. Understanding the motives for which they rate poorly can help you figure out their weaknesses, and this will give you something to exploit if you want to manipulate or influence them.

For example, if the person is non-reactive in the face of aggression, it could mean that their 'vengeance' motivation is on the lower end of the spectrum, and so they are less likely to come after you if you do something to set them off.

Depending on the reason why you are psychoanalyzing the person, any deduction you make can either be positive or negative information. In some cases, the reason people want to understand others is that they have vested interests. More often than not, it could be they are trying to figure out the person's motivations because they are romantically interested in them, and they want to know if they are compatible. If that's the case for you, you can go into your web browser and type in "Reiss Motivation Profile Test." You will find different free-to-use websites that have been set up as resources for people who want to have a better understanding of their own motivations. Take the test, then compare your most dominant motivations with those of the person you are psychoanalyzing, and try to figure out if the two of you will make a good pair.

Now that you know how to psychoanalyze people let's look at how you can use the information that you have gathered in a way that brings you maximum utility without putting you in an awkward position with the person that you are analyzing. First, when you are using the information to influence the person, don't make it obvious to them that you have been analyzing them. People get spooked when they realize that you are spending a lot of time creating some kind of psychological profile of them. No one wants their privacy invaded, or their trust violated, and whether you are dealing with a partner in a relationship, your child, a colleague, or a friend, they are going to start treating everything you do with total suspicion if they find out. By all means, don't go bragging about your psychoanalysis skills. Remember that the whole point is to be able to influence the person on a subconscious level, and if you bring this information into their conscious awareness, they'll definitely have a negative reaction, and it will ruin all your hard work. If, as part of your influencing strategy, you feel that you must reveal to the person some profound insight that you discovered about them, make it sound like a guess. Use phrases such as, "It seems to me that you are acting this way because..." or "I think maybe the reason you feel this way is that..." You want it to seem as though you have come up with some kind of clever insight—not that your knowledge stems from studying the person.

Now, if you have read widely on psychology and psychoanalysis, you may have come across some terms that, when used to describe people, could be construed as pejorative. In fact, most of the words that are used in clinical psychology are arguably insulting because they have negative connotations in everyday conversations. For example, you can't go around telling people that they are "narcissists," no matter what kind of evidence you have, and no matter how convinced you are of this fact. The one thing to draw from what you have learned about subliminal psychology is that subtlety is the key to success when you want to influence people without their knowledge.

Chapter 9: Use Words to Steer People However You Like

Words are extremely powerful. If you are a student of history in any capacity, you are probably familiar with the great speeches of leaders, rebels, and revolutionaries who incited people to action and ended up altering the course of generations. These remarkable people, whether they were kings or civil rights leaders, were able to do what they did, not because they were strong, powerful, or had infinite resources—they were able to do so using the power of words.

You can use words to steer people in whatever way that you like—all you have to do is pick the right words and present them the right way. The first thing you need to learn to master the art of influencing people using words is the concept of framing.

Framing

Framing refers to the act of presenting a story or a narrative in a way that suits your agenda, or in a way that gives you the upper hand in a situation. Even if you are conveying the same exact idea as someone else, the way you frame your idea has an impact on how your audience will receive it.

Framing is not about deception; sure, it can involve certain lies of omissions whenever necessary, but in most cases, it's really about stating facts from the point of view that does you the least harm or offers you the most utility.

The easiest way to explain the concept of framing is by looking at the difference between optimists and pessimists. We are often told that optimists have a "glass half full" outlook and pessimists have a "glass half empty" outlook when dealing with the exact same situation.

This is a classic example of framing; the optimist and the pessimist are looking at the glass and coming up with objectively accurate observations, but they are framing the observation differently. None of them is lying, but if they are recounting the facts to the same audience, they are going to elicit different reactions altogether.

Framing is a way for you to give meaning to things, events, or even actions, in such a way as to influence the way other people will ultimately perceive those things, events, or actions. Politicians use framing all the time with the aim of sensationalizing certain issues to get the electorate to react in an emotional way, often to their own benefit. Companies and even government agencies also do it all the time to influence public perceptions.

The "framing effect" is recognized as a cognitive bias that exists in all of us. It is defined as the tendency of people to make decisions when faced with options, based on how those options are presented to them semantically. This bias is deeply ingrained in all of us—in fact, the "framing effect" is responsible for some of the most important decisions we make in our lives.

Think of courtroom proceedings. In most cases, the judge and the jury are given two competing narratives of the same events, and they get to decide what version is the right one. The attorney will try to present her client in the best possible light, while the prosecutor (or opposing counsel) will try to do the exact opposite. Even if they are operating from the same set of facts, the way each one frames the case affects the outcome.

If you want to successfully steer people in whatever way that you like through framing, you have to prepare your narrative as any good attorney would. In order to be convincing, your ideas have to be coherent and articulate. You also have to set the right context so the people you want to influence can see things from your perspective.

If you work in sales, or your job involves pitching to clients, you can use framing to gain the upper hand in every meeting you attend. Your aim is to shape the perceptions and assumptions that inform the way your clients make decisions.

First, you have to present your product or service in a positive frame. Second, you have to present your competitor's products and services in a less favorable frame. Third, you have to create a sense of urgency, to make the client feel he has to act immediately.

These three steps may sound simple, but they are used in different iterations every day by business leaders, politicians, salespeople, suitors; pretty much everyone who wants to influence someone's choice.

When you use framing to influence others, there is one crucial tip you need to internalize: positive frames work better than negative frames. That is because positive frames generally elicit

95

positive feelings, while negative frames have a way of eliciting negative feelings.

Therefore, when you frame a narrative in a positive way, you are likely to get the people you are targeting to be more proactive and to take on more risks, but if you frame your narrative using negative language, people are more likely to be reactive, defensive, or to become more risk-averse.

When you create a sense of urgency in either case, it will have the effect of amplifying the positive or negative feelings that you have planted in the person you are trying to influence.

To help you understand the difference between positive and negative frames, think of two doctors who are trying to get their patients to eat healthily. The first doctor tells his patient, "If you want to live longer, you should cut down on the bacon." The second doctor tells his patient, "If you don't want to die, you should cut down on the bacon."

These two doctors are saying the same thing, but the first one is using a positive frame to convey his message while the second one is using a negative frame to do the same. Which one of them is more likely to get to his patient?

Well, according to studies that compared the rate of compliance to doctors' orders, those patients who were presented with a positive frame were more likely to follow the orders than those who were presented with a negative frame. So, to be more effective in steering people to do what you want using framing, you will get the best results if you decide to use a positive frame. People like to feel that they have a choice on different matters, and a negative frame will sound to them like coercion or threats.

As you use framing to influence people, you also have to remember that consistency is key. When you create a certain frame with the aim of influencing a person, you have to make sure that you stick with that narrative. If you switch things along the way, it is going to cause cognitive dissonance in the person, and he/she will decide to exercise his/her own perceptions and assumptions instead of basing the decision on your frame.

Asking "Yes" Questions

Apart from framing, you can also use words to steer people by asking "Yes" questions. Since you can't control the response that a person is going to give in a specific situation, you can use words in a very deliberate way to make the person feel obligated to give you an affirmative response. There are 2 different kinds of "yes" questions that we are going to talk about in this section; the literal "yes" question and the figurative "yes" question.

The first kind of "yes" question, as we have mentioned is the literal kind. In this instance, if you are trying to influence a person to do a certain thing, you start by getting him/her to say yes to a number of other less important things so the "Yes" response becomes sort of a pattern for that person.

The idea here is that once you get the person to start saying yes, they are more likely to agree to other things in a progressive and incremental way until they finally agree to what it is you wanted in the first place.

In sales, this technique is referred to as the "yes ladder," and it's a form of neuro-linguistic programming. It is based on the fact that people are naturally conditioned to stay consistent in their actions, words, and even their attitudes. So, when a person says "yes" to something small, in his/her mind, that is a form of commitment which he/she is going to try to stick to.

If you ask them to commit to something else that is similar to the first thing but slightly more crucial, they will say "yes" again because saying no will be contrary to their previous response. When you ask for a third thing, and they agree to it, they are now locked into a pattern, and it's up to you to keep steering them onwards.

You have to be careful how you do this. You could get someone into the "yes ladder," but remember that it's a ladder for a reason. You have to take it step-by-step so that the person is comfortable. If you make a sudden leap forward and ask for something that is too drastic, your scheme is highly likely to fail. Try to make the increments as small as possible.

The "yes ladder" is used to influence people almost everywhere. Even you might have used it without realizing what it was. Think of how most relationships start. You meet the individual in some kind of social setting and exchange some pleasantries. You subsequently meet them a few times later, and each time, the conversation gets a bit longer as you get more familiar with each other.

You then ask the person out. This is a form of "yes ladder" that plays out naturally, but it can help to explain how you can use words to steer people however you like by getting them to agree to a small thing. In this case, the first "yes" can be a mere "hello."

The "yes ladder" is used by salespeople to lock in customers, by philanthropic organizations to solicit for contributions, by pickup artists to seduce girls, and even by websites to get you to buy products and subscribe to services.

Car salesmen will start by getting you to agree to take a test drive. Philanthropic organizations may start by asking you to retweet their message or wear a ribbon. Pickup artists will start by convincing a girl to accept a free drink. Websites will start by asking you to agree to sign up for a free newsletter.

All these people and entities know that once they get you say that first "yes," they now have some considerable level of control over the situation. All that is left is for them to keep pushing, ever so slightly, and the rest of the dominoes will fall.

The second kinds of "yes" questions, as we have mentioned, are figurative. In this case, it's not about programming the person to answer affirmatively; it is about controlling the way the person can respond to your question.

For example, let's say that you are pitching an idea to a client or presenting options to a customer. You work hard on your presentation, and when you finally present it to the client, he turns you down right away.

This happens in most cases because you have presented the client with only one option, which means, that he can logically either accept that option or turn it down. You have a 50/50 chance of getting a "yes" or a "no."

Supposing, however, that instead of just presenting a single option to the client, you come up with 2 or three options. That will fundamentally change the way your client will perceive the decision that he has to make. With only one option, the question that's running in the mind of the client is, "Do I like this?" However, when the client has multiple options to pick from, the question that runs in his mind is, "Which one of these do I like?"

It all goes back to the perception of freedom. With one choice, the client won't feel like he has a choice at all, so he will exercise his liberty by turning your down. However, with multiple choices, the client will recalibrate his thinking, and he will start comparing the merits and demerits of each of the options you've put at his disposal.

This kind of "yes" question can be used in many other situations to your advantage. Your child comes down the stair in the morning, and you ask him, "Do you want a bowl of cereal for breakfast?" Since you have presented him with just one option, he could try to bargain and demand something that you don't have time to make.

However, if you ask him, "Do you want cereal or toast for breakfast today?" it immediately registers in his mind that pancakes are not on the menu, and he is more likely to say yes either cereal or toast.

Speech Fluidity

In order to steer people in whatever way that you like using just your words, you have to be good at delivery. You have to talk in a way that is convincing. That means that you need to practice speech fluidity. Fluid speech refers to a manner of speaking that makes one appear more confident and authoritative.

There is a difference between fluent speech and fluid speech. The first is about mastery of the language that one is speaking, but the second one is about mastery of delivery when one is communicating a specific idea. Being fluent doesn't guarantee that you will also be fluid in your manner of speaking. Fluidity means you talk in a way that is precise and clear, and that you convey conviction.

Most of us tend to use certain interjections when we talk and to use phrases that imply hesitation. If you keep saying "uhm" as you talk, it can be good for the flow of the conversation, but it tells the other person that you are unsure of what you are saying. Since your aim is to steer the person to see things from your point of view, the "uhms" only serves to erode the person's confidence in what you are saying.

The same goes for people who like to say things like "I mean" or "like." These words are very common conversation fillers, but when you use them, they make you seem less certain and less confident, and as a result, you will be less persuasive. In order to be truly persuasive, as well as to be effective in steering people with just your words, you have to drop all the ubiquitous filler words that you use, and you have to be more confident and direct in your manner of speaking.

Repeating Someone's Name

When you are trying to steer someone one way or another during the conversation, it helps if you repeat their name frequently. Names are very powerful tools when you are trying to persuade people or to control the way they perceive you. If you are in a group and you mention someone's name, they'll turn towards you and pay attention. We have all been conditioned to respond this way when our names are mentioned.

Our parents start calling us by our names long before we even learn how to talk, and then everyone else follows suit. Our grandparents, aunts, uncles, siblings, friends, and teachers reinforce the neural network in our brains further. This way, our names become permanent tags anyone can use to get our attention.

When we frequently call people by their names, it makes them pay attention to us, but it also makes them take notice of the fact that we are paying attention to them. In effect, it makes things personal. So if you are asking someone to do you a favor and you drop his name several times during your talk, it makes them more likely to comply with your request, because that request feels more personal.

When a person gives you their name, it effectively means that they are allowing you to think of them as individuals, not as total strangers. In other words, they are inviting you into their lives. When you meet someone for the second time, and you indicate that you remember their name, it creates a rapport between the two of you, because, in their subconscious minds, they realize they are important enough to you because you are able to recall their names.

If you want to be good at steering people, however, you like, you have to be good at learning their names. If you are dealing with clients, you have to remember their names and their voices; most of them will be impressed if, when they call your offices, you remember just who they are.

Apart from repeating someone's name, the way you say the name also has a bearing on how effective you will be at steering them to do what you want. The tone with which you say someone's name can indicate to them how you feel, and it can also influence how they'll respond to the request that you are making. Just like the name itself, the tone with which the name is uttered has also been well calibrated in the person's brain; everyone knows what it sounds like when their name is pronounced in anger because everyone has had their parents, family members, or friends yell at them in anger at some point. So, the way you pronounce someone's name will elicit a certain emotional response in them.

Think of two people trying to get someone else to go along with their ideas. The first person says, "I think option A is better than option B. What do you think?" The second person says, "Option A is better than option B. Don't you think so, Jane?"

The second person has a better chance of getting "Jane" to see things his way for two reasons; the first reason is that he seems more confident in his conviction that Option A is the right way to go. While the first guy says, "I think," the second guy doesn't express a hint of doubt in what he says.

Secondly, the second person refers to "Jane" by name, which makes things personal, so she is less likely to make her own objective judgment and more likely to defer to his judgment.

In personal relationships, it might be more endearing to use someone's informal name or their nicknames if you want to steer them in whatever way that you like. If it's someone you are dating, you could find out his/her childhood nickname and use it to prime him/her during conversations.

Word Associations

There are certain words that are associated with certain core ideas in most people's minds, so if you bring them up during conversations, you can prime a person and steer him/her to do what you want. Saying someone's name could be seen as a form of word association technique because it works pretty much the same way, but in this section, we will be looking at the words the work almost universally in all the people that hear them. Word associations can be used to steer both individuals and groups of people.

The word "you" is strongly associated with the self, and with the freedom of choice, so it works very well when you are trying to convince a person or groups of people to take certain actions. The word "you," as well as common variations like "your," can be used to make someone feel connected to something.

Next to someone's name, the word "you" is the most used when it comes to grabbing people's attention. What's even better is that it works on everyone, including total strangers. If you say, "Hey, you!" in a crowded room, everyone will pay attention and try to figure out if you are talking to them.

In sales and marketing, people are encouraged to use the words "you" and "your" as frequently as possible. Think of two real estate agents giving tours of houses they are looking to sell. The first agent says things like, "This is the kitchen, and it has marble countertops," while the second one says, "This will be your kitchen, and you'll have marble countertops." The two are conveying the same idea, and it can even be argued that the first one is more accurate in his/her use of grammar.

However, the second real estate agent is a much better salesperson because, throughout the tour, he/she primes you to picture yourself as the owner of the house. This makes you more likely to make a purchase.

The word "Imagine" can also be used to steer people to be more suggestible and compliant. When you hear someone say, "Imagine," your brain is engaged in a different way than it ordinarily is. "Imagine" primes you to use your creative side, and it engages your inner child.

It awakens your sense of wonder so that instead of thinking of things in empirical terms, you start opening yourself up to things you would normally assume are beyond the realm of what's possible. It makes you see things in a more magical way, so you are no longer limited by cold hard logic.

When you ask someone to imagine themselves as the owner of a brand new Ferrari, they will indulge you, because they know that imagination costs nothing. Whether you are a salesperson, an employee making a project proposal to the bosses, a guy trying to convince a girl to go out on a date, or a parent trying to get a child to study harder at school, the word "imagine" can be a powerful tool if you use it correctly.

Asking someone to imagine something doesn't change their reality or yours, for that matter, but it does something very important—it shifts the scales of their expectations. Imagination makes people lower their guard, and it opens their minds to different expectations altogether. With imagination, everything is possible.

With the word imagine, a realtor can get a couple to think of a rundown house as their future home. An entrepreneur can get an investor to think of a non-existent company as a blue-chip investment. A broke young man can get a girl to think of him as a future husband.

The next time you want to steer someone in a certain way, just ask them to imagine whatever possibility you are proposing. Their imagination will do most of the work for you.

The word "free" is one of the most effective words in the English language when you want to steer people to do something you want. People love free things. Very few people ever stop to consider the implication of whatever it is you are offering, because, in their minds, they know they are not paying for it.

In the context of any business, offering something for free will increase the chances that potential customers will take the first step towards engaging with a product or service that you are offering. However, if you put a cash value on the same product or service, your prospective customers will want to wait and see the value in what you are offering before they try it out.

The word free is used everywhere in marketing, and in as much as most of us find it annoying, we still respond positively towards it. We take free samples of products, and we try out online subscriptions services when we are allowed to use them for free for a limited period. In the supermarket, we are more likely to pick up products with "20% free extra volume" or those with "buy 2 get 1 free" labels. For salespeople, offering freebies is one of the best ways to hook people in.

In your personal life, you can get people to do lots of things by offering them something for free. If you want your friends to sacrifice their weekend plans and spend their Saturday painting your apartment, offer them "free" pizza and beer. It will make them feel like they are getting free refreshments, so the whole thing will feel more like a "cool hangout" than manual labor.

When you want your kid to do his chores, instead of telling him when to do it, ask him to do it on his "free time." It will make him feel like he has the freedom and flexibility to control the situation, and he is more likely to comply with your request.

Chapter 10: The Art of Lying and Identification

As you try to influence people's subconscious minds, you will have to deal with lying in one of two ways. First, you may find yourself in a position where you need to tell a convincing lie. In order to help you with that, we will discuss the art of lying. Secondly, you will need to tell when other people are lying to you so you can turn the situation around to your benefit. To that end, we will discuss techniques that you can use to identify and to detect other people's falsehoods.

Telling a Convincing Lie

Everyone lies. Lying is something that we all start doing at a very young age, and the fact is, without it, we would all be embroiled in a lot of petty and unnecessary conflicts. If you have to lie, then let's show you how to do it well.

First, you have to plan your lie. Psychologists have long understood that lying takes a lot more mental energy than telling the truth. So, if you have the luxury of time, you should use it to plan out your lie so you take as much mental effort as possible out of the lie before you actually have to tell it.

It's much easier, and much more convincing when you bend the truth instead of making up your lies from scratch. A lie that is grounded on truth is inherently much more believable. For instance, let's you are going somewhere, and you want to lie to someone by telling them that you were at a party.

If you swing by that party on the way to where you really want to go, you won't have to overcome much cognitive dissonance at the time when you tell a lie, because technically, it won't be a total lie. Swinging by the party should also be helpful should you find yourself in a position where you have to provide extra details, or if you are somehow forced to produce a witness who saw you there.

You want your lie to be believable, so, as you make up your story, tell a lie to yourself, and then try to look at it as objectively as possible and ask yourself if you would believe it. If you can't convince yourself that it's believable, you can be certain the other person won't believe it either.

You should also try to look at it from the other person's perspective, and try to predict what kinds of questions he/she might ask. You want to make sure your story doesn't have any gaping holes.

For example, if you lie about going to the library when you are at a party, someone who knows you well is going to be suspicious if, for the time she has known you, she's never pegged you as the kind of person who hangs out at the library.

Don't lie about something that is out of character for you; a lie like that will unravel pretty fast when it's put under scrutiny. You should also consider the personality of the person to whom you are telling a lie. People tend to believe the things they want to be true, and if you understand someone's personality, you can create a lie that is tailor-made for him/her to believe.

You should then practice telling a lie. Think of yourself as an actor learning the lines to a script. Practice in front of a mirror if you can. Go through the lie and make sure you have your details straight. If you fail to practice, you are more likely to be caught off-guard with an unexpected line of inquiry, and this could force you to make something up on the spot and to destroy your whole narrative.

If you are going to tell a lie that is particularly consequential, it could help if you used an audio or video recorder so that you can play it back, analyze it, and identify any hesitations or awkward mannerisms that could cause the other person to suspect something is amiss (of course, if you make a recording, you have to destroy it afterward; you can't leave evidence lying around).

As you create your story and as you rehearse it, you have to try as much as possible not to involve other people. Unless you have no other choice, don't bring others into it — the chances of getting caught increases exponentially with each additional person that you involve.

You may have close friends who are willing to lie for you, but you have to understand that no matter how close you are, they won't be as invested in the lie as you are.

Don't use your friends as alibis to help sell your lie. If your friend is in a position where she is likely to be asked to corroborate your story, don't give her a complex plotline. For example, you could tell your friend just to say, "I have no idea" when asked about your whereabouts.

After you have nailed down every aspect of your plan, you'll now have to tell a lie. Now, whether or not you feel ready, you have to understand that confidence is the key. Tell a lie as if you believe it. If you don't believe it, the other guy won't.

If you feel hesitation or guilt, you can counter those feelings by rationalizing; convince yourself you are lying not just for your own good, but for the other person's good as well. Are you lying about having an affair? Convince yourself that the lie will save your partner from emotional distress and heartbreak. Are you lying to your parents about sneaking out to a party? Convince yourself that they need the lie because they'll die of worry if they knew the truth. If you look at it that way, the lie is actually an act of compassion on your part. Do everything to sustain your confidence throughout.

As you tell a lie, you have to keep it short. Now, as you plan the lie, you will have to figure out a lot of details so that follow-up questions don't catch you off-guard. This, however, creates a problem when it's time to tell a lie. Because you have so many details at the tip of your tongue, and you are worried about forgetting some of them. You'll be tempted to spew them out all out once so as to lay everything on the table. That, however, is how liars get caught.

What you need to do is provide the least amount of details possible with each question that the other person asks. Only answer the question that has been asked, nothing more, and nothing less. Wait to hear the question in its entirety before you answer; if you retort quickly, you might think the question is headed one way only to find out later that it was going somewhere else, and then the other person will start wondering why you are acting so weird.

It's also important to hold back unnecessary details because many things don't sound out loud the same way they sound in our heads. You might think you have created a coherent thought, but when you say it out loud, you realize you included information that sends out a clear red flag.

For example, let's say you are late for work, and your boss asks, "Why are you late?" The simple answer is, "Sorry, got caught up in traffic." If he is more curious, he will ask which route you took, how long you were stuck there, and so on.

However, if you respond to the question with, "Sorry, I was on my way—but unfortunately, the freeway was backed all the way to exit six due to the repairs they are doing on the stretch near the park," the boss will wonder why you had all that ready to go.

When you tell a lie, sometimes you will feel an urge just to quit and tell the truth. That's how your brain is wired. The truth is something that really happened, so you only have to engage your memories. The lie, however, involves the use of the creative part of your brain. So, when someone asks a question, the truth is the first thing that pops onto the tip of your tongue.

To keep the truth from popping out, you can try a simple trick that will boost your inhibitions. You can try to tell your lie with a full bladder. When your bladder is full, your brain will engage its inhibitions to try to hold it back.

Because you will be exercising self-control in one area, it will be easier for you to do it in other areas as well, including withholding the truth. So, when you are planning on meeting the person you are to lie to, you can drink water 45 minutes before the conversation.

As you tell your lie, you also have to make sure that you move your body in a natural manner. During casual conversations, we all have our body movements. However, when we lie, we tend to stiffen up because we are anxious.

As you tell your lie, try to use your hands and other parts of the body in the same way that you always do. You will feel a natural inclination to cover your mouth, throat, chest, to touch your head, or to put arms across your torso.

You have to make a conscious effort to keep yourself from showing any of these signs because if you are dealing with a person who is particularly intuitive, he/she might sense something is wrong.

You also have to get a sense of your facial expressions. Avoiding eye contact is a sign of deception, but also holding eye contact for long can indicate that you are overcompensating. Hold eye contact for a few seconds at a time, and then break it as naturally as possible. Awkward head movements, such as tilting your head on the side or bowing it down, is also a sign of deception, so you should watch against that.

Lies have aftermaths. Once you say them out loud to a person who is constantly in your life, you have to carry on as if that lie is the truth, and the events you made up are an actual part of your history.

Until such a time as you may decide to unveil the real story, you have to find ways to remember the exact details of the lie you told. You might want to write those details down somewhere secret and revisit them whenever you think the issue is about to come up again.

You also have to tie up the loose end if there are any. If you had to implicate someone else in your lie, make sure they are on the same page as soon as possible. In the age of the internet, you have to be careful about your social media pages, as well as those of the people you hang out with. One of your friends could post something that incriminates you long after the incident has passed. For example, if you told your boss you had a cold, and instead, you went to some kind of pop-culture convention with your friends, make sure you don't appear in the background of some of the photos they post online.

Also, try to avoid telling frequent lies, and only tell lies when you need to. The more lies you tell, the harder it is to keep track of all of them, and the higher the chances that you will mix up the details and trip up. Reduce the number of lies you tell, and reduce the number of people to whom you tell the lies.

Finally, don't let the person you lied to catch you on other lies. If that person discovers that you are a lair, he/she will start questioning everything else that you said before, and that will be the end of the road for your well-constructed lie.

How to Tell When Someone Is Lying to You

As we have already mentioned, when someone lies, there are some voice and body cues that could reveal that they are lying. If you pay attention to those signs, you can be able to tell with an extremely high degree of certainty when someone is lying to you.

The first thing you need to do when you are trying to decipher whether someone is lying is to start by asking questions that are neutral. When people are having casual conversations, and talking about ordinary things, there are no stakes at play, so people tend to act in a relaxed and normal way. They don't feel threatened, and they have no reason to lie about anything, so if you observe them in this state, you can be able to know what their baseline responses are like. You can talk about things like the weather, shared memories, etc.

You should pay very close attention to their eye movements, their facial expressions, their use of hand gestures, their posture, their tone of voice, the kinds of words they use, and the speed at which they are talking. If you can, try to make a mental note of the placement of their legs as well.

Once you have a fair understanding of their baseline behavior, it's time to shift the conversation from the neutral topics to the "hot topics." Look at how their body language changes. Notice any difference in their eye movements. Take a look at the facial expression they exhibit. Keep a keen eye on their hand movements, listen for changes in the tone of their voices, and listen for alterations in the structures of their sentences.

Some small changes in body language may be manifested because the person is a bit uncomfortable with the "hot topic," but it doesn't necessarily mean that they are lying. Lairs tend to exhibit signs that are fairly clear. They'll try to pull their bodies inward, because subconsciously, they are trying to make themselves feel a lot smaller, and therefore less noticeable to you.

They will often start to squirm, and they may hide their hands because their fingers are becoming a bit fidgety and their palms are starting to sweat, so they'll instinctively try to keep their hands out of sight. They may assume a shrugging posture, so pay attention to the position of their shoulders.

The clearest telltale signs of deception are the ones related to micro-expressions. Micro-expressions are facial expressions that occur in the split of a second. They are so fast that if you are not a keen observer, you could miss them. The ordinary facial expression can be faked, but micro expressions are impossible to fake because they occur on a subconscious level.

For example, when someone is lying about something, at the exact moment he hears the question, he is going to show micro-expressions of fear or anxiety. However, when the question hits his conscious mind, and he starts to process it, he will remember that he is trying to "keep up appearances," and he may put on a fake smile.

All this happens in a fairly quick progression, but to the astute observer, there is going to be a brief moment when the person's subconscious will tear through the façade, and reveal his real emotions. You just have to look closely to catch it when it happens.

When a person is lying, the following are the micro-expression cues that you should look out for: If it's a light-skinned person, you may be able to notice that their facial coloration changes ever so slightly. The skin will become a shade redder or pinker. This happens because when the person experiences the turbulent emotions related to deception, his heart rate will increase, and blood will pump a lot faster to the facial area. It's a physiological response that the person is unable to control (unless of course, he is a psychopath).

Other people will have flared nostrils for a moment, while others may bite their lower lip. Some people tend to perspire at a faster rate when they are lying, so, those beads of sweat might be the clue you are looking for (of course, you have to observe the person under neutral conditions to make sure that he isn't just sweaty by nature, or that it isn't because the AC in the room is broken). Some lairs will also blink at a faster rate than they do during neutral conversations.

When you notice these changes, usually, it's because there is an increase in brain activity. As we mentioned earlier in the chapter, it takes a lot more mental energy to lie than to tell the truth.

Now, let's look at the verbal signs of deception. Often, when someone lies, his tone of voice might change slightly. The tempo of their speech will also vary from the one they use when talking about neutral topics. Some might start to speak faster than normal (either because they are anxious, or because they want to get through the topic as fast as possible and get to something else). Some may talk slower than normal (this could indicate that they are making up the story as they go, and they are slowing down to engage their creative brains and to organize the thoughts in their head into a believable narrative).

You also have to examine the structure of the sentences they are using. When people lie, they start using sentence structures that are increasingly complex. That is because the brain is going into overdrive, trying to weave a narrative that is within the realm of plausibility. You'll notice they'll throw in unnecessary details into what they are saying, and they'll offer supplementary explanations you didn't ask for.

As a point of caution, don't jump to conclusions based on just one or two signs of deception. Try to see if there are clusters of cues; the more the cues, the higher the chances that the person is lying. When you see the first signs of deception, keep pushing the person, and keep observing them closely; you should only act after you are sure they are deceptive.

Chapter 11: Predicting Reactions

So far, we have discussed many techniques that can be used to influence people on a subconscious level. However, all those techniques will be useless to you if you are unable to predict with a certain degree of accuracy how the person you are trying to influence is going to react to your machinations.

You can't just fly blind when you are trying to make someone do your bidding. Sometimes, the stakes are too high, so you have to make sure that you are able to monitor the progression of whatever machinations you have set in motion. You also have to be a few steps ahead of the person you are trying to influence. Hence, accurately predicting reactions is very crucial.

The first thing you need to understand about the nature of people's reactions is that it's based on emotions and not logic. Reactions are based on emotion because, in the hierarchy of things in the human brain, emotions are more primal than logic.

People react because they "feel" and not because they "think." When you ask someone why they have made a certain decision, they are going to tell you that it "felt right." If you ask them why they believe one version of events and not another, they are going to say that one account "feels true." Even when people say that their reasons for reacting in certain ways are purely logical, there is always an emotional component in those reasons. In fact, for most people, the reaction will be purely emotional, and the logical part of it will come later when they are rationalizing their actions.

That's just what excuses are—rationalizations for reactions that occurred as a result of emotional decision making. Every time you hear someone give an excuse that sounds flimsy, look back at the reactions that they are trying to explain away, and it will all be plain to see. You can tell exactly what emotion led to that choice. If you have spent enough time with someone, and you have seen him react in different situations, you might be able to tell that a similar reaction is coming if he starts expressing the same emotions that he did during a previous incident.

The good news for you, as you try to predict people's reactions, is that everyone has habits which are deeply ingrained in them, and are hard to break. People tend to fall into certain patterns when it comes to behavior in general, and to the way they react. People will subconsciously go back to their bad behavior even if it has caused them considerable harm in the past. For better or worse, they tend to stick with their patterns.

This has something to do with the way the brain works and how it stores memory and other information. For example, let's say that as a child, a person would throw a tantrum whenever they felt uncomfortable. Their parents would then give them the attention they were hoping for. Because this behavior guaranteed a favorable outcome for them at that time, it became wired into them.

The brain forms a neural network that stores this emotional reaction, and every time they experience a stimulus that's related to that neural network (in this case, when someone makes them feel uncomfortable) the same reaction is triggered. Unless the person has made a conscious effort to unlearn this bad habit, it will stick with him, even in adulthood. The manifestation may be a little different, but the underlying emotional reaction will be the same one.

When someone has a specific emotional reaction to a specific set of circumstances, that reaction stays the same unless it is addressed. A man who reacts by yelling and screaming will keep doing it unless external circumstances force him to stop. It could be that the people around him will call him out on his bad habit, and he will then decide to see a therapist about it or to make an effort towards self-improvement. If no one ever tells him what he is doing is wrong, or if he never fails to get what he wants despite his bad habits, it will never occur to him it's unusual.

Even if someone is getting professional help, breaking habits can be pretty difficult, so you can be certain the habit loops a person exhibits today will be the same ones he will exhibit tomorrow or next week.

Before you assume that someone's behavior will stay constant, you should pay attention to make sure that no major change has occurred in the person's life in the time that you have known them. People tend to break their habits during the times when their lives are chaotic.

For example, a person who always eats healthy foods may break that good habit and start eating junk food if she is going through emotional turmoil (a breakup, loss of a job, loss of a loved one, etc.). A student who performs well in class keeps doing so unless her home situation changes.

The point is that major change can affect someone's emotional stability, and it can, therefore, interfere with their brain's ability to fire up the same neural network that it did before. So, if you want to predict someone's reaction, and you are attuned to their emotions and their habits, make sure that there is no major "interfering factor" that can affect the accuracy of your prediction. Just to be clear, the change has to be something big; minor changes in one's life won't have that much of an interfering effect on the person's usual reactions.

For a person's behavioral patterns and habits to change, they have to want to change. In as much as someone else can call them out on a bad habit, the only way they are going to change is when they themselves acknowledge there is a problem.

This means that when you observe someone's reactions, and you detect a pattern, you should also look at the people who have any influence over the person's life, and try to figure out if they are trying to prevail on that person to change his behavior. If they are, you should keep a keen eye on how he reacts to their efforts. If he is receptive, hold off on making a conclusion, and wait to see what happens.

If it's a person that you are invested in, and you want to help them change their habits, the more effective strategy would be to make them think the idea for the change was theirs; this will make them more likely to commit to improving themselves.

Sometimes, to accurately predict a person's reactions, you have to factor in their environment. We all react in different ways depending on where we are, even if the reaction is triggered by the same stimulus. If you accidentally bump into someone within an office building, you are both likely to say "sorry" to each other, and then keep walking. If you bump into the same guy in the street, however, his reaction (and maybe even your reaction) is going to be a lot more aggressive.

There are also certain emotional reactions that a person might exhibit, which are specific to the circumstances that they are in at the moment, but are likely to change should the person's circumstances change. For example, an employee who feels underpaid may react in a grumpy and uncooperative way, when criticized by the boss, but when his salary is increased, he may exhibit a warmer reaction. A parent may react in a cranky way, but that could be temporary, and she might mellow out when she gets a less stressful job.

You have to figure out which reactions are ingrained habits, and which ones are based on prevailing circumstance. If you observe an emotional reaction in someone and you want to use it as a basis for predicting her reactions in the future, make sure there aren't any special conditions at the moment that could contribute to that reaction being more pronounced.

You have to remember that in as much as you can use your observation of past reactions to predict future reactions, people can surprise you, so don't completely bank on your past observations.

Historical information is helpful when predicting reactions, but you also have to build skills that can help you make predictions based on observations that you are making in real time.

Reactions, especially those based on strong emotions, tend to happen in a series of steps, and if you are paying attention to the person, you may see the earlier signs of a specific reaction and use it to figure out where things are going.

So far in the book, we have stressed the importance of learning to pay attention to people's verbal and non-verbal cues. Here, we will stress your need to practice that skill but for a different reason. Since emotional expressions tend to progress through specific steps, reading people's facial expressions, listening to their tonal variations, and observing shifts in their body language and position, can tell you when something is about to happen.

The good news is that you can sharpen your observation skills even during your downtime. When you watch TV or movies, pay keen attention to the faces of the actors, and try to figure out what they are going to do or say next based on the expressions on their faces. Even if those people on the screen are acting, their portrayal of emotional reactions are fairly good, and watching them can help you understand the way the face morphs and how body language changes when someone is starting to feel particular emotions.

Body language indicates how someone is about to react. Supposing you are asking someone for a favor, and you notice that he is starting to shift his face away from you; this could indicate that the person is disinterested in offering you the help that you need, and he is inclined to turn you down. You may be able to salvage the situation by changing your tact before he blurts out loud that he can't help you.

As you pay attention to body language, try to notice if it's closed or open. If the body language signs indicate that a person is relaxed and that his body position is open and facing in your general direction, it could mean that he is responding positively to whatever request you are making of him.

If, on the other hand, he is crossing his arm or his legs, or that he has set up an object that acts as some sort of barrier between the two of you, it could indicate that he is uncomfortable, and that could mean that he won't respond positively to whatever influence plan you are using on him (it could also mean that he has certain reservations, so you can try to address any concerns he might have and keep watching his body language to see if anything changes).

Sometimes, you can predict someone's reaction by paying attention to the words they are saying and trying to read between the lines. The reason many people don't see verbal outbursts coming is that they fail really listen to what the other person is saying in the moments leading up to the outburst.

Instead of planning what you are going to say next in your head, focus on the words, tone of voice, hesitations, and any other thing in the other person's voice. Something might clue you in on the fact it's not a good time to make the request you are about to make.

You can also predict what a person does next, or how he/she will react by taking a look at the position of their legs. Compared to all other body parts, legs are perhaps the most accurate indicators of a person's intentions.

The subconscious mind primes the legs to face the direction in which the person wants to go at that moment. If the person wants to walk away from you, his legs may point towards the door. If your date isn't enjoying her time with you, her legs might point in the direction of the exit. If a colleague is sitting at a different table from yours at a cafeteria and her legs are pointing towards you, it could be that she wants to come over and sit with you.

So far, the reaction prediction criteria we have looked at are those that are universal. You could use them to predict anyone's reaction in a general sense. However, to refine your prediction and to increase your accuracy, it could help if you gathered all you the personal information you can about the individual whose reactions you want to predict.

Habits and behavioral pattern are unique to the individual, but predicting a specific person's reactions goes far beyond that. You need to be able to know what his/her passions are. Figure out what the person likes and what she dislikes.

As you interact with the person on a regular basis, when they tell you that they like something, make a mental of the things they claim to like, and their tone of voice and body language cues at the moment they make that claim. When they say that they dislike certain things, make a note of all those things as well. This is crucial because people are passionate about the things they like and the things they hate. The tone of voice and body language can tell you how deep that passion goes.

For example, let's say someone speaks passionately about a certain sports team he likes, and you take note of that. The next time you are with him, and someone says something to disparage that team; you can be able to predict the emotional reaction the person might have.

You can also predict a person's reactions by noticing the things that he/she pays attention to. This is particularly important, not only for prediction purposes but also if you want to elicit that reaction. This is a very simple trick to comprehend; all you have to do is be observant. In fact, you have probably already used it a few times in your life.

For example, you are walking down the street with your girlfriend, and you notice that she is particularly interested in a certain handbag on a store window, you'll know that it would probably be a great gift for her. The next time you want to elicit a happy reaction (maybe you want her in a good mood so she can do you a certain favor), you can go back to the store and buy her the bag.

Sometimes, being able to predict a person's reactions can help you protect them from ending up exhibiting that reaction and suffering as a result. When your partner or your roommate is worried about an upcoming medical procedure, you can predict that he/she won't react well if a medical drama comes on TV, so you could save him/her the distress by turning on a different channel. Sometimes, it's just about putting yourself in the other person's shoes.

You can predict a person's reactions in specific contexts by figuring out what he/she is sensitive about. People have sensitivities that are unique to them (or to demographics to which they belong). These sensitivities are often referred to as "triggers." Due to their unique social or cultural experiences, some people might be scared of certain things. For other people, being in specific situations can put them on edge. They may also hold certain things dear to them, and they may be willing to "overreact" in order to protect those things. If you spend enough time with someone, you will catch on, and you will be in a unique position to predict their reactions in these special circumstances.

Conclusion

Thank you for making it through to the end of *Subliminal Psychology: Learn How to Influence People's Unconscious Mind to Do Anything You Want with Subliminal Persuasion and Dark NLP in Relationships, Parenting, and at Work*! I hope you have learned valuable techniques that can help improve your life by increasing your chances of getting what you want out of the people you interact with.

The next step is to start practicing these skills so that you master them by the time you need to use them. Remember that subliminal influence techniques and NLP techniques need to be deployed expertly, so without adequate practice, you could do something wrong and bring your target's attention to what you are doing. Hence, be extremely cautious—and don't start using these techniques without thinking things all the way through. Every time you want to use them on someone, create a well-thought-out plan. It's also important for me to address the issue of ethics. Influencing people isn't unethical at all—because everyone does it. On the other hand, influencing people on a subconscious level can be problematic if the person doing it has malicious intentions. Mastering subliminal psychology is like having a superpower, so it's up to you to decide whether to use your powers for good or evil.

Made in the USA
Monee, IL
16 May 2022

96503223R00079